PLANNING FOR INTEGRATED SYSTEMS AND TECHNOLOGIES

A How-To-Do-It Manual for Librarians

John M. Cohn, Ann L. Kelsey, and Keith Michael Fiels

HOW-TO-DO-IT MANUALS FOR LIBRARIANS

NUMBER 111

NEAL-SCHUMAN PUBLISHERS, INC.
New York, London

Published by Neal-Schuman Publishers, Inc.
100 Varick Street
New York, NY 10013

Printed and bound in the United States of America.

Library of Congress Cataloging-in-Publication Data

Cohn, John M.
    Planning for integrated systems and technologies : a how-to-do-it manual
for librarians / John M. Cohn, Ann L. Kelsey, and Keith Michael Fiels.
        p. cm. — (How-to-do-it manuals for librarians ; no. 111)
    Includes bibliographical references and index.
    ISBN 1-55570-421-2 (alk. paper)
    1. Integrated library systems (Computer systems)—Handbooks, manu-
als, etc. 2. Libraries—Automation—Planning—Handbooks, manuals, etc.
3. Small libraries—Automation—Planning—Handbooks, manuals, etc.
I. Kelsey, Ann L. II. Fiels, Keith Michael. III. Title. IV. How-to-do-it manuals
for libraries ; no. 111.

Z678.93.I57 C64 2001
025'.00285—dc21

                                                    2001044043

CONTENTS

LIST OF FIGURES

ACKNOWLEDGMENTS

The authors wish to express their appreciation to Philip McNulty of the Metro Boston Library Network, Deidre Brennan of the Boston Public Library, and Elizabeth Thomsen of NOBLE (the North of Boston Library Exchange) who read the manuscript and whose thoughtful suggestions made this book even better.

The authors also wish to express their appreciation to Tina Kelsey of Whippany, New Jersey, for her contributions to the creation of this work.

PREFACE

Planning for Integrated Systems and Technologies: A How-To-Do-It Manual for Librarians is the successor to *Planning for Automation: A How-To-Do-It Manual for Librarians, second edition,* published in 1997. The first edition appeared in 1992. The title of this completely new work reflects the expanded and updated focus of this volume, as well as the enormous changes technology has brought to our libraries over the past dozen years.

Planning for Integrated Systems and Technologies: A How-To-Do-It Manual for Librarians is intended to guide any library in planning for the introduction of an integrated library system or migrating from an existing system to a new one. We cover issues ranging from initial data collection needed for the preplanning stage to the process of actually implementing a system. First we emphasize the contribution careful and systematic planning makes to a successful outcome of your implementation efforts. Then we provide the nitty-gritty details you need to know to ensure a successful outcome of your efforts. Thus, we have devoted individual chapters to database preparation, the importance of standards, and other narrow, but vital, subjects.

We define an "integrated system" as one that computerizes a multiplicity of library functions using one common database. While this definition, which we first used in *Planning for Automation,* is still technically accurate, technologies in general and library systems in particular have evolved to the point where such a definition is certainly incomplete, if not antiquated. It suggests a focus on using computers where previously you did things manually; and, while that is no small consideration for a library that is acquiring its first system, the scope and potential of today's systems far exceed such a limited vision. Today's integrated systems offer much more than a common database for both user and librarian. These compelling ideas will be discussed at greater length in the "Introduction" as well as in subsequent chapters.

Planning for Integrated Systems and Technologies: A How-To-Do-It Manual for Librarians is designed to be current, useful, and simple to use. We have employed a convenient format and presented generous numbers of figures and checklists to demonstrate our points clearly. All the material strive to address the myriad needs librarians face today. Key issues include:

- how integrated systems are "evolving" to enable access to resources on the World Wide Web and to information in new formats

- changes in technologies and options that are open to today's library
- system migration and replacement
- latest possibilities now just becoming visible on most librarians' radar, such as the "application service provider" model for maintaining systems
- new standards that include references and explanations of new and emerging standards, including those for electronic books

Some issues are covered extensively, others more briefly. For readers who may want additional information about specific topics, annotated lists of Sources are included at the end of each chapter. There are various interesting citations, many of innovative Web sites, that we urge you to explore. The sources selected for these lists deal with the subject material in specific, direct, and practical ways; many of them contain references and bibliographies that may also be of interest. All citations include annotations.

The "Introduction" considers the issue of how the ongoing changes in technology are changing our perception not only of library *systems* but of libraries themselves. Part I, "Planning for Library Systems: Developing and Sustaining a Basic Technology Plan," places the system implementation effort—whether for a first-time system or a migration—in the context of planning generally and in developing, specifically, a technology plan. Chapters in Part I discuss how to collect data and develop a library profile in preparation for implementing technology, how to assess and identify institutional needs and priorities, how to go about writing and updating a technology plan, and approaches for evaluating and amending your plan. One chapter presents a model process for developing a basic strategic plan.

Part II, "Selecting and Implementing Integrated Library Systems," begins with an analysis of how systems are evolving to incorporate new technologies and to meet changing user expectations. Subsequent chapters review options for implementing systems, translating needs and priorities into system specifications, evaluating proposals from system vendors and selecting a system, and the issues involved with putting your system into place and properly maintaining it. A chapter on training deals with both staff and public training and, in the case of system migrations, *re*-training.

Part III, "Planning Your In-House Collection Databases," is principally concerned with the steps involved in creating and maintaining the library's own, in-house, machine-readable databases. The chapters cover retrospective conversion of manual files, maintaining the bibliographic database, weeding collections, bar coding collections, and the MARC standard for bibliographic description. The final chapter in Part III discusses a wide and growing assortment of crucial standards that pertain both to material formats and to your library's computer network. The "Conclusion" offers comments on the life cycle of integrated systems and on the benefits of good planning for improved library services.

To wind things up, there is an appendix that considers the consultant relationship—finding, selecting, and working with consultants who are often retained by libraries to assist with identifying priorities and evaluating technological options. One section focuses specifically on ethical issues involved when using a consultant for a system selection project.

Planning for Integrated Systems and Technologies is a hands-on book, one that is written to provide librarians in medium-sized and smaller libraries of all types with practical advice on planning technology projects and implementing systems in a sensible and systematic manner. As readers familiar with mastering challenges of the computer revolution know, what appears daunting and overwhelming at first blush becomes manageable when it is demystified. Understanding the issues and getting organized are the keys to a successful technology effort, either for the first time or when replacing an existing system. *Planning for Integrated Systems and Technologies* provides the concepts and the tools for such an effort.

INTRODUCTION

WHAT DOES "AUTOMATING THE LIBRARY" MEAN TODAY?

Until the early 1990s, "automating the library," as it pertained to library *systems*, meant computerizing the traditional library functions of circulation, cataloging, the public catalog, acquisitions, and serials check-in using the library's database as the foundation. Systems were fundamentally local, with the emphasis on controlling and accessing resources within a discrete library or defined network of libraries, not on accessing remote databases or library catalogs. Systems were text-based, with no graphics, sound, or multimedia capability. They ran on powerful super-microcomputers, minicomputers, or even mainframe computers.

During the 1990s, however, library automation underwent a transformation that reflected changing definitions of library service in general and access to resources in particular. Rapid technological change forced a comprehensive re-examination of what automating the library really meant—not just for libraries but for the library user as well.

During this period, the library user entered cyberspace, and came to expect the local information provider—the school, public, college, or special library—to provide the launching pad. Accordingly, the purpose and scope of the library's automated, *integrated* system was broadened to do more than just computerize manual or paper-based routines. Systems had to connect through the local library or network of libraries into systems of other vendors, far-flung networks, full-content databases, and, of course, the Internet. "Accessibility" was re-defined to include the ability to obtain resources and information in all formats wherever it was located, from anywhere, at any time, day or night.

Thus, "automating the library" no longer refers only to computerizing operations in a discrete, physical place. It has assumed a wider frame of reference—namely that of enabling the library user to reach beyond what is "merely" local to an information and knowledge base that is truly global and interconnected.

EVOLVING EXPECTATIONS AND THE CHANGING NATURE OF LIBRARY SYSTEMS

The changes described above are often represented by the concept of the library as a "gateway." We use that term throughout this book and it remains a valid portrayal of the library as a launching pad or "doorway" to resources in other locations.

However, the concept of a library system as a gateway is no longer sufficient. That is because the expectations of library users have grown to include more than just retrieving materials from other places. As we explain in this book, particularly in Chapter 7, users now expect to be able to manipulate what they find and interact with it in new and customizable ways. This begins with the interface between them and the information, which users now expect will be a common interface enabling a seamless organizing of the material from wherever it may come and regardless of the source. Users see themselves as adding value to what they find by (legally) manipulating the information content and customizing the library system's functionality for their own purposes. A catalog is no longer just a list of resources in a given place; it is a database that can be merged with or linked to other databases and other resources in other places.

Accordingly, the vendors of library systems are forging alliances with content providers of all kinds in order to adapt their systems to these new expectations. We provide examples of these in Chapter 7; however, the number and variety of such arrangements will no doubt have expanded greatly by the time this volume is published. New technologies, and their imaginative exploitation by both up-and-coming and older companies, are creating the potential for new, enhanced, and expanded capabilities and services offered through or as an integral part of "local," integrated systems.

THE PLANNING IMPERATIVE

What all this re-affirms for your library, of course, is that, regardless of size and with perhaps only limited or static funding, you must, as always, select and manage space, collections, systems, and other information resources to meet the needs of your users. The rapid growth in user expectations makes decision-making all the more challenging, and points to the importance of sustained planning as the engine of managed change.

In the year 2000, over 15,000 libraries purchased or upgraded integrated library systems in this country. Given the fact that planning usually occurs prior to the securing of resources in an annual budget, this suggests that at least 30,000 libraries are currently in some stage of planning or implementation at any particular point, and the actual number is undoubtedly much higher.

As we suggested in the 2nd edition, the big difference between the present and the past is that *the library is no longer the only information game in town*. There are at least two examples of this phenomenon:

1. Many users perceive the Internet and the untold number of "sites" it links worldwide as the alternative to libraries. How many times do we hear people ask: "Why do we need libraries now that we have the Web?"
2. Many of the content providers referred to above are developing products and services that are geared directly to the end-user, not to the library as an intermediary. The library becomes an after-thought, a secondary market rather than the primary customer.

So, while libraries may understand the limitations of the World Wide Web and the complexities of identifying, harvesting, and organizing information from diverse sources, our users do not always have that same understanding. At one level, it is hard to persuade a youngster who may have a computer at home that exceeds the capacity of those in an under-funded local public library that the library is a "player" in the information game. At another level, a corporate manager contending with shrinking budgetary options may see the library as an expendable commodity, particularly when she can access "everything" from her desktop workstation or a laptop.

There are no easy, certain, or guaranteed-successful responses to these challenges. However, given such increased complexities and heightened levels of expectation, libraries must learn all the more how to plan effectively for technology and for the deployment of systems and services. A crystal ball is not necessary, and there is little mystery involved. It is entirely a matter of building upon what you already know about your library, using tools that are readily at hand, and, most importantly, involving *from the beginning* the people who are your library's "stakeholders" and who will live with the consequences of your decisions: your staff and users.

SOURCES

Anderson, Carol L., and Robert Hauptman. 1993. *Technology and Information Services: Challenges for the 1990s*. Norwood, NJ: Ablex Publishing.
Parts of the book are no longer timely given its publication date. However, Chapter 14 (pp. 197-210) — "Technology and Information Services in the 21st Century: The Recent Past Points the Way to the Future" — offers useful insights on integrating technologies and on how technologies are changing libraries as organizations and librarians as professionals. The chapter discusses the importance of strategic planning in dealing with technology issues.

New York State Education Department. "Doorways to Information in the 21st Century: Every New York Library an Electronic Doorway Library." 1998 [Online]. Available: www.nysl.nysed.gov/libdev/edl/thirdpln.htm [2001, March 11].
This report "provides New Yorkers with a statewide plan for technology-based library services," carrying forward earlier plans to the years from 1998 to 2000. It reflects the concept of the library as a doorway or gateway to the wider world of information resources beyond the library's walls.

Odlyzko, Andrew. "Silicon Dreams and Silicon Bricks: The Continuing Evolution of Libraries." Revised draft, May, 1997 [Online]. Available: www.research.att.com/~amo/doc/silicon.dreams.txt [2001, February 23].
This article offers a personal look at the future of libraries in the digital age. The author places libraries of all types in their historical context, describing how different types of libraries are being impacted by changing technology and how libraries are responding. He includes a discussion of Amazon.com and other "competitors" to libraries in the information marketplace. Some will take issue with his conclusions, particularly concerning his "low-tech" solutions that he believes will keep libraries going as they "evolve." However, it's a provocative look at some of the issues that are raised in this "Introduction."

Saffady, William. 1999. *Introduction to Automation for Librarians*. 4th ed. Chicago: American Library Association.
This edition carries forward the state-of-the-art survey that characterized previous editions and that offered an orientation to the basics in the field, including, but not limited to, integrated library systems. "An understanding of automation will allow you to allocate resources, make staffing decisions, and provide services to patrons more efficiently."

"Technology Awareness Resources." 2000 [Online]. Available: www.rwc.uc.edu/academic/libmedia/lt/techawareness.html [2001, March 23].

Part of the challenge is simply keeping up with the changing technology scene. Prepared by the Library/Media Services Department of Raymond Walters College, University of Cincinnati, this site offers lists of library-oriented periodicals with a technological focus, electronic discussion groups, newsletters, listservs, dictionaries and glossaries, how-to guides, product reviews and vendor information, and continuing education opportunities—all geared to library technology.

PART I

PLANNING FOR LIBRARY SYSTEMS: DEVELOPING AND SUSTAINING A BASIC TECHNOLOGY PLAN

Yogi Berra is quoted as having said, "You had better watch out if you don't know where you're going, because you might just get there." The process by which we get where we want to go is called planning. Simply put, *planning is the process by which we make decisions about what to do and outline how we will do it.*

In today's library environment, planning is more critical than ever. Information technology has expanded rapidly to include a wide array of systems and services that allow a library to manage locally created information and to access information scattered across the globe. It is vital to develop a *basic technology plan* as a first step in identifying which automated systems and services will best meet user needs and fulfill the mission of the library.

Given the rapidly changing nature of library technology, a *strategic planning* approach is particularly useful in developing plans for automation and technology. Strategic planning, which has become the planning method of choice for many organizations in almost every field of endeavor, focuses on:

- identifying key environmental issues influencing the library—for example, initiatives within a parent organization or the availability of new technology—and the library's strategic responses to these issues
- defining a vision of service that describes ultimate outcomes but provides for flexibility in achieving these outcomes

1

In short, strategic planning is most useful in situations where you can describe *what* you want to accomplish but are not yet sure *how* to go about it. In the context of this book, strategic planning will lead to the development of a technology plan through which you can make decisions about specific systems or technologies that will best support your service program.

Developing a basic technology plan involves eight steps:

1. assessing existing technology and services
2. assessing the environment and client needs
3. establishing priorities
4. developing your mission, goals, and objectives for action
5. developing a preliminary budget proposal to implement the plan
6. evaluating your plan's accomplishments
7. redefining your priorities, as necessary
8. updating and revising your plan

Remember that your local planning process can—and should—be tailored to accommodate your resources (that is to say, your time) and your needs. For this reason, along with Chapters 1 to 4 and 6 that take you through each of the steps involved in developing and updating a basic technology plan, Chapter 5 presents a simplified, two-day process for undertaking a basic strategic analysis. There is no "perfect" planning process, however—only one that works!

1 THE UNDERLYING IMPORTANCE OF PLANNING FOR FIRST-TIME SYSTEMS AND SYSTEM MIGRATIONS

HOW DO YOU DEVELOP A PLAN?

In the early nineties, many libraries had yet to select their first integrated online library system. Planning efforts were focused on shifting from manual to automated check-out and check-in and creating machine-readable representations of shelflists through retrospective conversion projects. Some very early adopters were moving to second-generation systems, but more libraries were automating for the first time than were migrating from one automated system to another.

In the ensuing decade, however, a sea change began to occur. As more and more libraries were reaching the end of the life cycle of their first automated system, they began to consider migrating to an enhanced version of their current system or to an entirely different system. This is because the first systems of many libraries were created to access and manage primarily locally held resources, especially *print* resources. Today, libraries must be able to access a wide array of resources and databases, in all formats and available anywhere. Users expect seamless access across system platforms to wherever such resources are located.

Accordingly, hardware and software products have changed drastically in the last few years. In terms of overall functionality, libraries expect systems that offer:

- comprehensive connectivity to all kinds of systems, including older, "legacy" systems
- the ability to establish and control external links to remote resources

- the ability to customize the system locally
- seamless movement between and among functions within the system
- search engine power and flexibility
- support for all recognized standards
- compatibility with the World Wide Web
- the ability to support both MARC and non-MARC formats

What remains the common denominator between first-time system selection and system migration, however, is the importance of planning. A needs assessment program resulting in a solid, well-conceived technology plan is as vital for a library's successful migration from one system to another as for a library implementing a system for the first time, or for other technology-based initiatives. A well thought-out planning process enables a library to approach migration not as a frantic means of escaping from a legacy system on its last legs, but rather as an opportunity to provide enhanced services to its user community.

Much of the planning process described in this book will apply equally to libraries acquiring systems for the first time and libraries migrating from one system to another. While the framework remains the same, however, specifics may differ dramatically. The library's challenge is to apply the concepts of planning within the context of the systems environment in which it exists. A well-conceived plan will address specific technology issues that are mirror images of each other.

Figure 1–1 illustrates this by listing a representative sampling of comparative issues for libraries implementing an integrated system for the first time and for libraries migrating from an older automated system. The resolution of these issues will benefit from a coherent well-structured planning document.

Figure 1–1 Planning Issues: First-Time System and System Migration	
First-Time	**Migration**
• Shelflist cleanup and conversion	• Extraction and movement of data files
• Workflow changes from manual to automated environment	• Workflow changes from old to new software
• Increased staff productivity	• Increased user productivity
• Staff and user training	• Staff and user retraining
• First-time bar coding	• Replacement of nonstandard bar codes

SOURCES

Agnew, Grace, and Toni Lambert. 1996. *Online System Migration Guide* (LITA Monographs 7). Chicago: Library and Information Technology Association and American Library Association.
This 47-page guide offers a "practical checklist for online system migration." Four sections cover data preparation for export, hardware and facilities preparation (including telecommunications), preparing library staff, and vendor support issues.

Cortez, Edwin M., and Tom Smorch. 1993. *Planning Second Generation Automated Library Systems*. The Greenwood Library Management Collection. Westport, Conn.: Greenwood Press.
"In charting the procurement process, the book indicates how to migrate the library's database. The book . . . takes into account the experience of those libraries that have already automated and are now considering migration to more powerful automated library systems."

"Integrated Library System Migration Study." Steering Committee. Report and Recommendations. December 18, 1997 [Online]. Available: www.lib.uiowa.edu/oasis/ils/report_12.18.97/report_12.18.97_txt.html [2001, February 10].
This report by a committee charged to "investigate the issues related to replacing the current (integrated library) system" at the University of Iowa in 1996 offers an informative review of trends in library system development. It places the migration process firmly in a planning context, discussing stakeholders, market trends, strategic issues (what other institutions are doing), and system functionality.

Kelly, Margaret. "System and Data Migration in Libraries." Updated October

26, 2000 [Online]. Available: www.personal.umich.edu/~megrust/migration. htm [2001, May 30].

This survey of the literature covers the time period from 1995 to 2000. The annotated citations are divided into three categories: general overviews, "how-we-did-it," and short articles from *Library Systems Newsletter*. The annotations are detailed, and the author has chosen citations that cover the system migration process in all types of libraries. Common themes include the fact that data migration from one system to another can be problematic, since data structures differ and vendors are not always equipped with the software and utilities needed to successfully move data sets from another vendor's system into their own environment. Problems that occur can result in additional or hidden costs that may have not been evident during the selection process.

Muirhead, Graeme. "If It Ain't Broke, Fix It Anyway." *Library Technology* 2, no. 4 (August 1997). [Online]. Available: www.sbu.ac.uk/litc/lt/1997/ news183.html [1997, September 29].

This article by the editor of the book on migration listed below "seeks to raise the morale of those facing change." The emphasis is on "automation as process," that is, helping the organization and its staff cope with change through open communication, consultation, and planning.

————, ed. 1997. *Planning and Implementing Successful System Migrations*. London: Library Association Publishing.

This volume presents case studies to aid those involved in library migrations. Chapters deal with why migration was undertaken, functional requirements for new systems, selection, and installation.

Nicholas, Margareta. "What Is, Where Is the Horizon?: Technology Planning and Budgeting as Part of the ILMS Replacement Process." March 23, 2000 [Online]. www.library.unisa.edu.au/papers/codi2000.htm [2001, March 31].

This paper reviews planning and budgeting strategies needed to complete an integrated system upgrade. The context is upgrading from an older Dynix system to newer systems, but the strategies discussed are applicable to any situation. The author discusses the importance of planning, upgrade options, and the procurement process as it applies to all upgrade options. The paper considers the training needs of staff, the psychological impact of change, and other "neglected aspects" of an upgrade project.

Ralston, Rick, et al. 1999. "With Feet Planted Firmly in Mid-Air: Staff Training for Automation System Migration." *The Serials Librarian* 36, no. 3/4: 407–413.

This article discusses "practical ideas and suggestions for training serials staff to deal with a new system and the transition process." Through a look at one specific area of library operations, the article presents material on the migration process from initial planning through implementation to daily operations under a new system.

2 DESCRIBING EXISTING LIBRARY SERVICES AND TECHNOLOGY

The first step in developing a technology plan is to describe existing library services, automated systems, and electronic accessibility. What services are we providing in each of the basic functional areas of library service, and how much are we providing? What technologies are we currently using, and what service functions do these technologies provide?

HOW ARE LIBRARY FUNCTIONS REDEFINED IN AN ELECTRONIC AGE?

It is important to think about what we do and what we have in the broadest possible terms. In our rapidly changing times, we must think creatively about traditional functions and services—acquisitions, cataloging, the public catalog, circulation, reference—and make our planning horizon as wide as possible.

A basic model of library services in an electronic environment will help organize your planning efforts at each step in the process. Based loosely on work by David Penniman that we found particularly useful, our model remains relevant today.

Our model consists of four basic functions of libraries in an electronic age:

1. providing access to the content of local resources (for example, books, periodicals, media, electronic resources) that are part of the library's collection
2. offering gateway or portal access to remote resources (for example, books, periodicals, media, electronic resources and so on), including the ability to obtain copies in print and electronic formats
3. facilitating off-site electronic access to local and remote resources from users' homes, offices, and schools
4. providing access to human assistance in locating information

(*Note*: We define "portal" as an entry point or starting site for the World Wide Web, combining a mixture of content and services.)

Each of these functions is described in more detail in Figure 2–1.

Figure 2–1 Library Functions in an Electronic Age

Function	Description
Access to the content of local resources that are part of the library's collection—e.g., books, periodicals, media, electronic resources	Includes the shelving and display of hard copy and other library materials as well as accessing (via library workstations) an automated catalog containing bibliographic records, locally created electronic resources, and files created by external providers and stored locally. All files can be searched by author, title, subject, and other indexed descriptors.
Access via gateway or portal to remote resources (other collections of books, periodicals and other media, and external electronic resources) with the ability to obtain copies in print or electronic format	Encompasses accessing from library workstations those resources not residing at the local library. Users can search for information by author, title, subject, and other descriptors, which lead them to bibliographic records, abstracts, the full texts of documents, and other textual, graphic, and multimedia files. Materials are obtainable through online interlibrary loan request or via electronic transmission, with provision for copyright compliance and the secure transmission of billing information.
Electronic access to local and remote resources from off-site locations such as homes, offices, and schools	Includes direct access to local library systems via remote public workstations, telephone dial-up, or the Internet.
Access to human assistance in locating information	This function is provided by on-site trained librarians who serve as the human interface to all information services, either in person or remotely via fax, electronic mail, video conferencing, online tutorials, real-time chat, or instant messaging.

COLLECTING AND ORGANIZING BASIC STATISTICAL DATA

One of the most important tools a planner needs is basic statistical information on the library and its operations. Whether you are setting priorities, preparing a preliminary cost estimate, providing information for an RFP—a Request for Proposal from a vendor—or calculating the storage requirements for your new system, you will find that the same basic data will be needed again and again.

The Basic Data Worksheet in Figure 2–2 provides a checklist of commonly needed data. Remember, if you do not have all of this information, you can develop reasonably good estimates by sampling a week or month in order to develop a projected annual figure. In the case of relatively static data, such as collections, reasonably good estimates can be developed by sampling a portion of the collection and extrapolating. For most planning purposes, an exact figure is neither necessary or worth the investment of resources that would be required.

Figure 2–2 Basic Data Worksheet

PRINT AND MEDIA COLLECTIONS
____ Number of nonfiction print book titles
____ Number of nonfiction volumes
____ Number of fiction print titles
____ Number of fiction volumes
____ Number of adult titles
____ Number of juvenile titles
____ Number of periodical, serial, or journal titles currently received
____ Number of periodical, serial, or journal titles retained but no longer currently received
____ Number of nonprint media items
____ Number of government documents
____ Number of uncataloged items (paperbacks, pamphlets, clipping files, and so on.)

CIRCULATION
____ Number of books circulated annually
____ Number of nonprint items circulated annually
____ Number of uncataloged items circulated annually
____ Number of holds processed annually
____ Number of overdue notices processed annually

PATRONS
____ Number of registered patrons/borrowers/users

ACQUISITIONS
____ Number of new items purchased annually
____ Percentage of items purchased through primary jobber
____ Percentage of items purchased directly from publishers
____ Number of standing orders

REFERENCE SERVICES
____ Number of reference transactions
____ Number of reference transactions involving use of e-mail
____ Number of searches performed using in-house reference databases
____ Number of searches performed using remote reference databases, including Internet resources
____ Number of electronic documents or files downloaded or printed

DOCUMENT DELIVERY SERVICES
____ Number of periodical articles requested from remote sources
____ Number of interlibrary loans requested
____ Number of interlibrary loans provided

Figure 2–2 *Continued*

ELECTRONIC RESOURCES

____ Number of electronic databases on CD-ROM

____ Number of electronic subscriptions to licensed databases

____ Number of fiction and nonfiction electronic book titles

____ Number of electronic journal subscriptions

____ Number of URLs/pages in library's Web site

____ Number of locally created electronic images (photos, maps, documents) in library's Web site

____ Number of locally created audio files in library's Web site

____ Number of locally created video files in library's Web site

REMOTE ACCESS

____ Number of "hits" on library Web page

____ Number of searches of library catalog from remote users

____ Number of searches performed using remote reference databases, including Internet resources, by remote users using library portal

____ Number of pages accessed by remote users via library portal

____ Number of electronic documents or files downloaded or printed by remote users

PHYSICAL INVENTORY

____ Number of staff workstations

____ Number of public workstations

____ Number of combined catalog/database/Internet workstations

____ Number of catalog/database-only workstations

____ Number of Internet-only workstations

DESCRIBING EXISTING TECHNOLOGIES IN THE LIBRARY

The next step in your planning process is to describe any existing technology being used by the library. The Basic Technology Assessment Worksheet organizes information on existing automated services, data files, software, and hardware (see Figure 2–3).

Hardware comprises the physical equipment that makes up an automated system, including the processor/server; storage devices such as floppy, hard and CD-ROM or DVD drives; telecommunications equipment such as modems and routers; and other peripherals such as printers and keyboards.

Software includes the electronic program applications that allow the hardware to perform a set of functions, such as tracking circulation or cataloging.

Data files are electronic files that contain information specific to the library, such as bibliographic records, abstracts, documents, patron files, statistical data, and Web pages.

Using the framework and functions given above, list those automated systems or services that are currently used in your library. What hardware does each run on? What software is employed? What data files, local or remote, are maintained or accessed on a regular basis? What kind of information do they contain and how many records are there?

It is a challenging process to develop a comprehensive, detailed inventory of existing technology and data files, but it will ultimately be worth the effort as you plan for new systems and services. It is equally important to organize your overview of systems in relation to the information access functions. This is important later in the process as you examine the possibility of consolidating single-function systems—the stand-alone CD-ROM reference workstation or a Windows-based catalog are examples—into more flexible, integrated systems.

Figure 2–3   Basic Technology Assessment Worksheet

Function	What automated services* are currently provided to support this function?	What hardware supports this service?	What data files currently exist to support this service?	What software supports this service?
Access to the content of local resources that are part of the library's collection, e.g., books, periodicals, media, electronic resources				
Access via gateway or portal to remote resources (other book and "virtual" collections) with the ability to obtain copies in print or electronic format				
Electronic access to local and remote resources from off-site locations such as homes, offices, and schools				
Access to human assistance in locating information				

Use a separate worksheet for each service.

SOURCES

Lynch, Clifford, and Hector Garcia-Molina. "Interoperability, Scaling, and the Digital Libraries Research Agenda: A Report on the May 18–19, 1995 IITA Digital Libraries Workshop." August 22, 1995 [Online]. Available: www-diglib.stanford.edu/diglib/pub/reports/iita-dlw/main.html#2 [2001, March 24].
This Web site is included here to make the point that even in this rapidly changing environment, the authors report that for workshop participants, "(t)here is . . . a very strong continuity between traditional library roles and missions and the objectives of digital library systems." They "emphasized that the traditional library institutional missions of collection development, collection organization, access, and preservation must extend to the digital library environment," and that "(d)igital libraries will be a component in the broader range of future library services. . . . "

Owen, J.S. Mackenzie. August, 1997. "The Future Role of Libraries in the Information Age" [Online]. Available: www.hum.uva.nl/bai/home/jmackenzie/pubs/Future%20role%20of%20libraries.htm [2001, February 23]
In much the same fashion as Penniman—cited below—Owen discusses the traditional function of libraries in the "information chain." He observes how that function is changing from that of a "clearinghouse" and service center for printed publications towards that of a "supplier of networked services for digital information resources" as well as a publisher of internal materials accessible via the Web. Owen refers to this role as "knowledge mediation" and describes the four S's of library service:
- Selection—selecting and acquiring materials in the marketplace
- Storage—maintaining publications through long-term care and preservation
- Service—making information resources available through consultation, lending, and document delivery
- Support—giving the user guidance and assistance

Penniman, W. David. 1987. "Tomorrow's Library Today." *Special Libraries* 78, no. 3 (Summer): 195–205.
The author reviews the (then) environment for libraries in business as well as in the public sector and offers strategies for extending library services without creating more "bricks and mortar." He describes his concept of an "information access station" that combines "the physical, electronic, and human elements of information delivery." The library functions described in this chapter are based upon the functions Penniman envisioned for his access stations.

3 ASSESSING NEEDS AND SETTING PRIORITIES

WHO NEEDS TO BE INVOLVED IN PLANNING?

Once data collection has been completed, planning can begin in earnest. Deciding who will be involved in the planning is as important as any other part of the process.

Stakeholders—those individuals who have a particular interest in the outcome of your automation efforts—should be involved in planning as much as possible. They may be internal—for example, individuals representing the different departments of your library—or external—perhaps individuals representing your parent organization or governing body—or lay persons from your community or clientele. If you are automating in cooperation with another library or libraries, participants should reflect the nature of the project.

You also want to make sure that the individuals you involve in planning will assist you in securing a favorable outcome. Users, for example, can help insure that your plans will reflect an improvement in services; representatives of your governing body or parent organization can help ensure support (and funding) for your plan.

A library will often form a planning or steering committee, made up of stakeholder representatives, that will meet regularly during the planning process. Eight to twelve persons seems to be the optimum size for such a group, although larger groups may be appropriate at certain points in the process (such as for the two-day activity described in Chapter 5).

EMPLOYING NEEDS-ASSESSMENT TECHNIQUES

A needs assessment essentially gathers information on what services users would like to have available from your library that they are not currently receiving. A needs assessment can be an elaborate, expensive process, or it can be as simple as a single session devoted to identifying services that should be provided or improved.

A needs assessment usually involves one or more of the following components:

- analyzing information on existing use
- distributing written user surveys
- holding focus groups, interviews, or informal discussions with users
- analyzing services provided by comparable or competitor libraries

Existing use patterns can help to identify areas of need. Highly used services may need to be further expanded, little-used services improved. Of particular benefit are any data you may gather on an ongoing basis regarding unfilled requests or user complaints.

Written surveys are frequently conducted as part of the needs-assessment process. While planning groups are frequently tempted to undertake extensive surveys, the results of these surveys can be difficult to translate into specific needs. A series of short surveys will often produce much higher response rates and can be developed at specific points in the needs-assessment or planning process to shed light on particular questions or issues.

Interviews or informal discussions with users can be very useful in identifying problems in existing services and systems or in discovering what your users really need but never thought to ask for. A more formal process, however, is to organize a focus group or groups. This technique consists of getting small groups of eight to twelve users together in a comfortable setting to discuss specific topics and talk about the library.

Focus groups are widely used to help generate the kind of information that is difficult to obtain using written surveys, including user perceptions and needs that users may find difficult to articulate. While the selection of focus group participants should include users, almost every library has some existing group that can be approached to participate in a focus group-type discus-

---

Figure 3–1 A Quick Guide to Conducting Focus Groups

Step 1: *Plan your focus group.*
Prepare an interview or discussion guide that states the objectives of the focus group and asks three to five questions. The questions should begin with a warm-up query, then move to more specific questions designed to elicit more detailed answers to your basic question.

Step 2: *Recruit your participants.*
Who is most likely to speak to the outcomes specified in your objectives? Who can best answer the questions in your interview guide? These are your participants.

Step 3: *Conduct the session.*
The session is conducted by a moderator, lasts 1.5 to 2 hours, and consists of three phases:

- establishing rapport with the group, structuring the rules of group interaction, and reviewing objectives
- stimulating intense discussion on relevant topics
- summarizing the group's responses to determine the extent of agreement

During the session, a note taker will record responses and areas of general agreement. The session may also be taped.

Step 4: *Writing up the results.*
A written report summarizes the results of the focus group based on the objectives of the session.

---

sion—for example, library friends, faculty members, or a corporate management team. Discussions of this type, whether formal or informal, should also be conducted with library staff. See Figure 3–1 for an outline of steps for conducting focus groups.

Although focus groups work best when an outside facilitator leads the discussion, many organizations now have access to individuals with focus group experience who may be available to work with you if you do not have funding available to hire a professional. It is also possible to conduct your own focus groups with a little assistance from resource people within your organization or faculty from a neighboring college.

Finally, another useful tool for identifying needs is to examine the programs and services of other libraries serving comparable user populations, with an emphasis on those libraries that have achieved recognition for their outstanding efforts. What services do they offer that your library does not?

A Basic Needs Assessment Worksheet, which can be used to summarize the findings of your needs-assessment activities, is given in Figure 3–2. Note that this worksheet encompasses the same functions as the Basic Technology Assessment Worksheet presented in Chapter 2.

IDENTIFYING PRIORITIES

Once you have completed your needs assessment, you have

- described how needs are being met or not met,
- identified possible approaches to meeting these needs, and,
- learned what the priorities are from the perspective of your stakeholders.

If your needs assessment has been successful, you should have identified one or more needs that you are not currently meeting. If you are lucky enough to have received such clear, articulated feedback from your users—and this does not always happen— any new services or service improvements requested should be considered as priority concerns.

In *Planning for Automation*, we discussed automation priorities largely in terms of user perceptions about needs that translated into the library . . .

- offering a new service based on computer technology;
- performing manual processes more efficiently by substituting technology, allowing staff to focus their efforts on more productive activities.

Today, users and other stakeholders are as likely to voice concerns that involve building on or extending existing services that involve fairly sophisticated technologies already available in the library. Some examples of this include:

- digitizing local history resources and making them accessible through the library's integrated system
- implementing "remote authentication" so that users who are off-site can access the library's electronic resources
- integrating a library's branch database into the main library's online catalog
- creating one coherent Web interface for the library's collections

Figure 3–2 Basic Needs Assessment Worksheet				
Function	How is this service* being provided currently?	What problems or limitations exist with the way this service is being provided?	Ideally, how should this service be provided?	What is the priority of this service based upon stakeholder input?
Access to the content of local resources that are part of the library's collection, e.g., books, periodicals, media, electronic resources				
Access via gateway or portal to remote resources (other book and "virtual" collections) with the ability to obtain copies in print or electronic format				
Electronic access to local and remote resources from off-site locations such as homes, offices, and schools				
Access to human assistance in locating information				

*Use a separate worksheet for each service.

- linking the library's serials control system to index databases in order to highlight citations relating to titles available in full text on site

Either way, your next step will be to relate expressed needs and concerns to existing library resources and technologies (from Chapter 2) and determine which library services should be automated or enhanced technologically and in what order of priority.

FROM IDENTIFYING PRIORITIES TO IMPLEMENTING THEM: A PLANNING CHECKLIST

Implementing your identified priorities requires evaluating them against each other and against your existing resources. If needs and priorities are clearly understood and placed in their proper context, they can be implemented in phases, allowing for more effective use of frequently scarce funding.

Here is a checklist to help organize this stage of your planning efforts.

A PLANNING CHECKLIST

❏ Based on your needs analysis, make a preliminary determination about which service priorities you would like to implement.

❏ Outline the current problems or needs that are characteristic of each service priority.

❏ With data from your Technology and Needs Assessment worksheets, identify the resources—human and material—that your library currently devotes to this service (if it is a service you currently provide). Some specific questions are:

   ❏ How much staff time is devoted to this function or service?

   ❏ How much space and equipment are used?

   ❏ What volume of activity is involved?

   ❏ How much does it currently cost to offer this service?

❏ Determine the relative importance of each service within your overall plan for library services.

❏ Do some preliminary research into what kinds of systems are available for each of the services you are considering implementing or enhancing with new technologies. Ask yourself:

   ❏ How much will these systems cost?

   ❏ What is your staff's ability to deal with these systems, taking into account their existing levels of technological expertise?

   ❏ How much staff time and how much of the library's financial resources can you devote to developing, implementing, and maintaining technologies to support these services? How much additional time and financial resources would be needed if they cannot be provided using existing resources?

   ❏ How will these systems free up staff and other resources or improve services to your users?

❏ Based upon all of the above, establish an implementation schedule or proposed plan and budget for each of your service priorities.

REDEFINING YOUR PRIORITIES

As you incorporate your service priorities and implementation plans into your overall technology plan, keep in mind that priorities change over time. Ongoing assessment and evaluation, discussed in Chapter 6, requires that your planning process not be a one-time undertaking. You must repeat the process periodically and continually reassess your priorities.

Consider the following:

- In the public library environment, population shifts, economic conditions, or community issues can impact your users or stakeholders and how they perceive the library's services.
- In the school and academic environments, increasing attention is being paid to assessing "outcomes" (how do we know that students are actually learning something in your information literacy course?) rather than "inputs" (how many books do you have on your shelves?).
- In higher education, the proliferation of distance-learning instruction is forcing libraries and learning resource centers to reevaluate how their service programs must be reconfigured to meet the needs of students who never set foot on campus.
- In the corporate world, mergers and takeovers can quickly change key players, who may bring very different ideas about how the information center can best meet their needs.

These scenarios point to the importance of always evaluating and reassessing service priorities. The library's overall service mission may remain essentially the same, but specific services and the technologies adopted to carry them out are both dynamic and subject to changing user expectations and needs.

SOURCES

Bremer, Suzanne W. 1994. *Long Range Planning: A How-To-Do-It Manual for Public Libraries*. New York: Neal-Schuman.
This book covers the planning process, with sections on getting organized, planning committees, taking inventory, setting goals and targeting objectives, and writing a plan. Concrete examples, timetables, worksheets, and checklists are included.

Fink, Arlene, and Jacqueline B. Kosecoff. 1998. *How to Conduct Surveys: A Step-by-Step Guide*. 2d ed. Thousand Oaks, Calif.: Sage Publications.
Very user friendly, this book covers the process planning and designing to analyzing and presenting findings. Includes many real world examples. Gives an overview of how to do various statistical analyses of survey data.

Greenbaum, Thomas L. 1997.*The Handbook for Focus Group Research*. 2d ed. San Francisco, Calif.: Jossey-Bass.
This book discusses focus groups—their planning, conducting, and reporting. While the book is geared to the marketing field, it does provide an overview of the technique and many examples of its use.

Krueger, Richard A., and Mary Anne Casey. 2000. *Focus Groups: A Practical Guide for Applied Research*. 3d ed. Thousand Oaks, Calif.: Sage Publishers.
The book provides instruction on the purposes and processes of focus group research. Particular attention is paid to the analysis and reporting of focus group results. The numerous examples will be especially useful to those who are just getting started.

New York State Teacher Resource and Computer Training Centers. "Focus Groups: An Overview." No date [Online]. Available: http://program evaluation.org/htmdocs/qcrse/focusgr.shtml [2001, February 23].
This Web site offers useful information on focus groups—when to use them, advantages and disadvantages, strategies for organizing them, questioning strategies, the difference between structured and unstructured groups, information-recording strategies, and how to analyze and communicate information coming out of focus groups.

Salant, Priscilla, and Don A. Dillman. 1994. *How to Conduct Your Own Survey*. New York: John Wiley & Sons.
This book discusses mail and telephone surveys as well as face-to-face surveys. It lays out ten steps for success in conducting a survey and then spends one chapter illustrating each of the steps. Gives advice augmented by both exemplary and poor examples.

Salzwedel, Beth A., and Ellen Wilson Green. 2000. "Planning and Marketing." *The Medical Library Association Guide to Managing Health Care Libraries*, edited by Ruth Holst, 37–54. New York: Neal-Schuman.

This chapter presents an excellent summary of the planning process, including sections on key planning steps, who's involved in planning, plan development and implementation, and the close relationship between the planning process and the marketing process. "Planning is the tool that allows the library to evolve its products and services in a systematic fashion, taking into account the types of information needed by library users as well as the best way to deliver it" (p. 37).

Sudman, Seymour, and Norman M. Bradburn. 1982. *Asking Questions: A Practical Guide to Questionnaire Design*. San Francisco: Jossey-Bass.
This book gives a detailed treatment of question design, with sections on the order and format of the questionnaire, the design of telephone and mail surveys, and a step-by-step questionnaire checklist.

4 WRITING AND UPDATING YOUR STRATEGIC TECHNOLOGY PLAN

Now that you have assessed your library's needs and identified and set your priorities, your final planning step is the actual writing of your technology plan.

Earlier, we talked about the importance of planning. In our book entitled *Writing and Updating Technology Plans* (Neal-Schuman, 2000), we discussed at length the significance of technology plans per se and how they can be organized, targeted, and written to serve the library's needs most effectively. This chapter will summarize the key elements of a library technology plan and the importance of keeping the plan current.

HOW DO LIBRARIES IDENTIFY THEIR MISSION, GOALS, OBJECTIVES, AND ACTIONS?

A technology plan should include the following components:

- a statement of the library's mission
- goals and objectives for the use of technology in fulfilling this mission
- activities required to accomplish these goals and objectives and their cost

The library's mission defines why the library exists, what it is, and what it does. Most libraries already have a mission statement, but they should revisit it in light of the impact of new and emerging information technologies. It is important that you understand the mission of your parent organization, that your plan support this mission, and that your parent organization understand and accept its mission.

In addition, your plan should conform as much as possible in format and structure to other planning documents within your organization. Basic elements found in most plans are:

- A *Statement of Purpose*. This phrase describes an articulated mission or overall vision that frames goals, objectives, and actions. For a library, such a statement is less likely to focus on technology as such and more likely to emphasize the acquisition, organization, distribution, and use of resources and the provision of services.
- *Goals*. These are broad statements of desired or intended long-term accomplishment based upon the statement of purpose. Technology-related goals include those that enhance services or allow new services to be offered. These would include increasing the effectiveness of existing services, such as cataloging, indexing, or circulation control; improving the ability to access information that is not currently available to users; or allowing information to be located or processed in new ways.
- *Objectives*. These are narrower assertions of desired or intended shorter-term accomplishments designed to achieve a goal. Objectives outline how or how much of the goal will be fulfilled in as concrete and specific a way as possible. If your goal is to provide access to a wide variety of databases, you will need a series of objectives indicating exactly how many, what type, and when you propose to make them available.
- *Actions*. These are measurable activities, often in a specific time frame, undertaken to achieve an objective. For the objectives just cited, your actions would detail when you will issue an RFP, select a particular index or full-text file, and make that index or file available.

The sidebar "Basic Components of a Technology Plan: An Illustration" on the following page offers an example of how each of these different elements may relate to one another.

A Technology Planning Worksheet (Figure 4–1) provides a format for developing goals, objectives, and actions for library technology in your library.

In developing your written plan, it is critical that your goals and objectives be as user-oriented as possible. What you want to do is less important than what the plan will accomplish for your users. Luckily, your needs-assessment work will help you to cast your plan with the user perspective in mind.

Basic Components of a Technology Plan:
An Illustration

Statement Of Purpose: .....to enhance and serve the community as a catalyst for and integrator of knowledge in all its forms

Goal: ....to maintain a state-of-the-art automated, integrated library system for the identification, organization, and delivery of information resources in all formats and wherever they may be located

Objective: ....to undertake a planning process for migrating the library from its current legacy system to a new integrated library system with the next 24 months

Action: ....to issue an RFP to selected vendors by the fourth quarter of the current year.

Figure 4–1 Technology Planning Worksheet

STATEMENT OF PURPOSE:

FUNCTION	GOAL*	OBJECTIVE*	ACTION*
Access to the content of local resources that are part of the library's collection, e.g., books, periodicals, media, electronic resources			
Access via gateway or portal to remote resources (other book and "virtual" collections) with the ability to obtain copies in print or electronic format			
Electronic access to local and remote resources from off-site locations such as homes, offices, and schools			
Access to human assistance in locating information			

*Use a separate worksheet for each goal, objective, and action statement, since each function is likely to generate multiple goals with multiple objectives and actions in turn.

PUTTING A PRICE TAG ON YOUR TECHNOLOGY PLAN

Since the emphasis in this book is planning for integrated library systems, the following discussion will center on that particular form of technology.

AUTOMATION COSTS

There are ten major cost elements involved in the installation and operation of an integrated system:

- planning and consulting costs
- purchase of system hardware and software
- purchase of network-specific hardware, software, and cabling
- telecommunications
- conversion of manual records into machine-readable form or processing of existing electronic data for use in the new system
- access, and subscriptions where appropriate, to external databases and systems
- Internet access
- ongoing operating costs
- additions to the system hardware and software
- initial and ongoing training for system operators and library staff

When the system is shared, it is standard practice to allocate these costs between libraries or among consortium members.

Planning and consulting costs include the direct (out-of-pocket) and indirect costs associated with getting started. You may need to hire a consultant to assist with long-range and technology planning and to involve the staff in preparing for and participating in all aspects of the automation endeavor. The costs of this process may not be immediately apparent, but remember the old adage: Time is money.

Initial purchase costs include acquiring the initial system hardware and software and of preparing a site or sites for the equipment.

- *Hardware* covers the server or servers, disk drives, workstations, printers, routers, switches, and other machine peripherals.
- *Software* covers the licensing of the system vendor's software providing the system's functionality—OPAC, circulation, acquisitions, and so on.
- *Site preparation* includes identifying space for the equipment and assuring proper room ventilation and, as necessary, air conditioning.
- *Vendor-provided training* costs must also be considered when the system is first installed, as well as the costs of connecting to the Internet.

Purchase of network-specific hardware, software, and cabling requires the design and implementation of a local area network (LAN) on which the system will run. This includes the selection of appropriate wiring, network architecture, a network operating system compatible with the system selected, and firewall hardware and software. Most integrated library systems now operate on LANs that not only provide access to local collections but also are gateways to the wider world of information available via the Internet.

PC workstations interlinked through Ethernet-based network interface cards using 10-Base 100 category 5 cabling wire are continuing to replace the "dumb," text-only terminals previously used by library systems. These local networks run through network operating systems, which must be compatible with both TCP/IP (Transmission Control Protocol/Internet Protocol) and with the operating system (for example, UNIX/LINUX, Windows NT/2000, Windows 98/ME) of the integrated systems selected.

Workstations connect to a server that in turn connects to a wider off-site network through high-speed, broadband digital lines provided by the telephone company or other service providers.

Telecommunications costs are no longer the concern only of shared systems or multibranch sites. All libraries must now factor in the costs of being a gateway to global information resources. In addition to telephone company line connections, there are the expenses associated with equipment, such as switches, routers, and hubs, to connect to the Internet and to the external databases of specific vendors. When a system is shared by multiple users at different sites, this equipment is also used to link up each site's local area network into a wide area network for access to the system's servers and workstations.

Through the Universal Service program (the *"e-rate"*), public and school libraries are eligible to receive discounts for the installation of wiring and telecommunications equipment, Internet service provider (ISP) costs, as well as ongoing telecommunications costs. Discounts are dependent upon the number of residents served by the library who live below the poverty level and can average about 50 percent of the library's telecommunications costs.

Conversion costs are those associated with the creation of machine-readable bibliographic, patron, and other records that will be used by the system. Conversion expenses include staff costs—yours or an outside contractor's—associated with inputting data, as well as the machine costs of the computer actually generating the new record. **Data migration** costs are incurred when moving from an old automated system to a new one. These costs include the processing of existing data such as cataloging records, patron records, and item records so that they can be used by the new system.

Databases and systems external to the library are now accessible through software gateways. These databases—as easily and transparently searchable as your own local catalog records—contain not only citations but also the full text of articles and books, pictures and other images, and audio and full-motion video. The cost of accessing these databases, including subscription and other fees, must now be factored into every library's technology budget.

Ongoing operating costs include hardware and software maintenance fees and costs for utilities, bar-code labels, miscellaneous supplies, and telecommunications. Major ongoing costs are the salaries and benefits of staff assigned or hired to manage and run the system. If the library contracts with outside firms to maintain all or part of the system, there are those costs as well. **Internet service provider costs** are another ongoing cost that must be included in your calculations.

Additions to the existing system may be required to maintain performance specifications, to accommodate new users, or to allow for additional functionality. In those cases where the addition of new users requires a system upgrade, the cost of the upgrade is often charged totally or in part to the new user(s).

Training costs extend beyond those costs associated with vendor-provided training on the integrated system. Typically, vendors expect their library clients to maintain certain levels of technological competency. For example, staff members being trained must be familiar with the Windows environment, while library staff who are the system operators must, at minimum, know how to install, maintain, and troubleshoot network servers and workstations. Libraries must be prepared to fund such training initially—and budget for the continuing education of both library staff and system operators.

If a system's costs are shared by two or more users, these costs may be divided equally or assigned on a proportional basis determined by a mutually agreed-upon formula.

In a consortium, the responsibility for some of these expenses is borne by the individual library (the purchase of local workstations, printers, and telecommunications devices) and others are borne by the consortium. These consortium expenses are then divided among the individual members as annual assessments through a cost allocation formula. Traditionally, cost allocation formulas have been developed based upon activity or usage levels, represented by such factors as circulation count, number of patrons, or system resources utilized. Formulas based on these criteria can be difficult to develop and maintain because they are based on variables that are subject to frequent change. An alternative is to develop a membership assessment based upon annual budgetary target goals determined by the participants or upon a formula driven by less subjective variables, such as the number of workstations operating on the system.

See "An Illustration of a Funding Formula for Consortia" and the accompanying Figure 4–2 (on pages 35–36).

DEVELOPING A PRELIMINARY BUDGET

Your technology plan should also include a proposed budget, which will be the basis for the preparation of your annual budget if you control available financial resources. If, as is more likely, needed resources are not under your control, the plan and budget will form the basis for a special request to your funding source. In the case of a public library, this will be a board of trustees and municipal or county government; in the case of a special or academic library, a department or division head, CEO, or chief academic or financial officer; in the case of a school library, a principal or superintendent.

The cost option information you gather in your planning will allow you to present general budget estimates for each proposed component of your plan and to document your cost proposal in detail as it is reviewed by your funding authorities.

The identification of technological options, discussed in greater detail elsewhere in this book, may involve a variety of activities:

- reading journals and other reference works
- having informal discussions or meetings with potential providers of services and systems
- visiting other libraries and talking with other librarians
- commissioning a consultant's report
- gathering information through the use of formal requests (RFI, RFQ) to vendors
- gathering information through the Web

In general, discussions with other librarians via telephone or online and, if necessary, visits to other libraries, are most useful in identifying realistic options and costs for your library. If a system or service is already in use by another, comparable library, you can glean how it will work in your library and how much it will cost. Keep in mind, however, that each variation in circumstances impacts the cost; the basic statistical profile you have prepared will make it easier to identify these differences as you examine systems in other libraries.

A consultant's report can be a valuable source of information on options and their approximate costs. Consultants are frequently used at this stage and are generally worth the investment if you can afford it. If you cannot afford to employ a consultant, you can still do a good job of identifying options and costs, and the extra time you spend gathering this information will increase your knowledge and understanding of the various technologies.

Once you have identified general options, your next step is to begin gathering more specific information from potential vendors. In addition to informal discussions and visits, there are two more formal mechanisms for gathering information from vendors in a more organized fashion: Request for Information (RFI) and Request for Quotation (RFQ). The RFI and RFQ are different from the Request for Proposal (RFP)—discussed in Chapter 9—in that they are shorter (RFIs are often one page) and request information on products and services. In the case of the RFI, you will be gathering information on specific system capabilities; for the RFQ, you will also be determining information on pricing. RFIs and RFQs are generally used in conjunction with, but usually should not replace, an RFP. In most publicly funded institutions, an RFP will be required for any purchase above a certain threshold amount, so an RFI or RFQ would be used in the early stages while developing a budget or funding request but prior to actual selection and purchase.

Finally, there is no guarantee that your funding source will give you the resources to implement your plan. You can be sure, however, that you are far less likely to receive new resources without a well-prepared and well-organized technology plan.

KEEPING YOUR TECHNOLOGY PLAN CURRENT

Keeping your plan current pertains to a number of important issues:

- Your technology plan should reflect the needs and expectations of your library's stakeholders. These needs and expectations change over time, and your ongoing planning process should keep abreast of the changes. Your technology plan—its objectives, actions, and perhaps even its goals—must be updated accordingly as part of the process.
- We are all aware of the rapid pace at which technology is evolving and impacting on our lives. We spend much of our time trying to understand it, manage it, and apply it productively. Plans must incorporate what is useful and relevant to the goals we are trying to achieve. We must remain alert both to new technologies and to how existing technologies are blending and converging to afford new opportunities for improved service.
- Technology plans are never merely wish lists or shopping lists. They represent a statement of intent, direction, and projected accomplishment. Those for whom plans are written, other than ourselves, for example, funding authorities, governing bodies, and upper management, may view technology plans in a changing light. Initially, they may perceive plans as providing the justification or rationale for substantial expenditures. In time, they may begin to look for indications that your plan is addressing the need to assess and evaluate what has been accomplished.

Thus, keeping your plan "current" means more than just acquiring the latest version of the Windows (or some other) operating system. It means ensuring that your plan is a "living" document—a dynamic statement of how technology is adopted and employed to carry forward the library's broader mission of service.

AN ILLUSTRATION OF A FUNDING FORMULA FOR CONSORTIA

In this model, library members of a consortium decide upon annual target goals to fund their anticipated needs. Then an assessment is developed based upon these target goals, with each participating member assessed cost shares according to the following formula:

Member share	25% of the target, divided by the number of participating libraries
Site share	25% of the target, divided by the number of participating library sites
Workstation share	50% of the target, divided by the number of active workstations

A library pays the member share x 1, the site share x 1 or more (for one or more branch library locations), and the workstation share x the number of workstations it is using on the system. Level of usage activity, library collection size, patron base, and so on are not factored into the equation.

ILLUSTRATION

For purposes of this illustration, assume 20 participating member libraries and 35 sites, with a total of 400 workstations. "Participation" means any library or group of libraries accessing the integrated system for whatever purpose.

Assume a target goal of $500,000. Thus:

Member share (25%):	$125,000/20 libraries = $6,250/ library
Site share (25%):	$125,000/35 sites = $3,571/ site
Workstation share (50%):	$250,000/400 workstations = $625/ workstation

Figure 4-2 illustrates how the assessments would work for three consortium members. Library A is a single library with no branch locations using 12 workstations; Library B is one library with one branch location using 20 workstations; and Group of Libraries is a group with four members using 50 workstations.

Figure 4–2 Allocation of Consortium Assessment

	Library A	Library B	Group of Libraries
Member share	$ 6,250.00	$ 6,250.00	$ 6,250.00
Site share	$ 3,571.00	$ 7,142.00	$ 14,284.00
Workstation share	$ 7,500.00	$ 12,500.00	$ 31,250.00
Total assessment:	$ 17,321.00	$ 25,892.00	$ 51,784.00

An analogy can be drawn to how automated systems were first perceived by many of those responsible for acquiring and implementing them. They were so expensive, you geared yourself up to buy a system—*once*. It would last forever. Only in time did we learn that systems often needed to be upgraded or replaced altogether within just a few short years. A technology plan is no different. You cannot write it once and expect to use it through the ages without amending it. Your plan must be reconsidered periodically to ensure its currency, its appropriateness, and its value to you and the library as a strategic instrument of change and achievement.

SOURCES

Bryson, John M. 1995. *Strategic Planning for Public and Nonprofit Organizations: A Guide to Strengthening and Sustaining Organizational Achievement*. Rev. ed. San Francisco: Jossey-Bass.

Bryson, John M., and Farnum K. Alston. 1996. *Creating and Implementing Your Strategic Plan: A Workbook for Public and Nonprofit Organizations*. San Francisco: Jossey-Bass.
This guide and accompanying workbook offer perhaps the most concise overviews available of strategic planning, with material on the context and process of strategic change and a ten-step process for strategic planning. Sections include, among others, agreeing on a process; identifying stakeholders; developing a mission and values; assessing the environment to identify strengths, weaknesses, opportunities, and threats; identifying strategic

issues; establishing an organizational vision for the future; developing an implementation process; and reassessing strategies. The workbook consists of worksheets for each step that take the user through the process of developing a plan.

Cohn, John M., Ann L. Kelsey, and Keith Michael Fiels. 2000. *Writing and Updating Technology Plans: A Guidebook with Sample Plans on CD-ROM.* New York: Neal-Schuman.
This book is designed to help librarians create, use, update, and evaluate detailed technology plans to meet organizational objectives or specific requirements such as the federal e-rate program. There is an appendix citing technology planning resources available on the Web and an accompanying CD-ROM with 50 technology plans for different kinds of libraries throughout the country.

Imhoff, Kathleen R.T. 1996 *Making the Most of New Technology: A How-To-Do-It Manual for Librarians.* New York: Neal-Schuman.
This volume "helps librarians improve library service to users by writing a technology plan; improving the technology selection decision-making process; understanding factors that can affect technology planning; and identifying the wide range of opportunities for improving information service that new technologies can offer." The book includes an "idea analysis worksheet" for use in the planning process.

Jacob, M.E.L. 1990. *Strategic Planning: A How-To-Do-It Manual for Librarians.* New York: Neal-Schuman.
"Chapters explain the variables that contribute to successful planning, including underlying assumptions, environmental considerations, strategic focus, and both personal and institutional values and priorities." Checklists, work forms, and examples are provided throughout the volume.

"Strategic Planning for Rotary Clubs of District 7850." May 2000 [Online]. Available: www.rotary-district–7850.org/Lbl_5160.htm [2001, February 26]. Although having nothing to do with libraries, this Rotary Club "How To" kit offers a nice review of the entire planning process in easy-to-comprehend language. Key concepts and definitions; basic steps; developing strategies, goals, and objectives; components of a plan; and implementation issues are all included. The site has some interesting figures, including a useful "Checklist for Planning Assessment" that is designed to measure the effectiveness of the entire planning process.

Tebbetts, Diane R. 2000. "The Costs of Information Technology and the Electronic Library." *Electronic Library* 18, no. 2, 127–136.
Noting that fast-paced developments require continual updating of hardware and software, the author discusses the impact of information technology requirements on the costs of today's "electronic library." Networking access consists of initial costs and recurring expenditures. Electronic content, training, and support demand ongoing expenditures, installations, and

upgrades. The article offers strategies for dealing with the need for continuous funding and long-term financing to keep up.

5 OUTLINING A MODEL TWO-DAY PROCESS FOR DEVELOPING A BASIC STRATEGIC PLAN

HOW CAN LIBRARIES ORGANIZE A BASIC PLANNING ACTIVITY?

One of the most effective methods of developing a basic strategic plan is by bringing a group together and working in a structured process. There are many ways of accomplishing this. This chapter proposes one such process—an intensive, straightforward approach to strategic planning that emphasizes four elements:

1. providing an opportunity for library stakeholders to articulate their ideas, hopes, and concerns in a structured, facilitated setting
2. identifying factors in the institution's operating environment likely to influence or impact any technology initiative
3. identifying perceptions and needs as they relate to library service
4. validating priorities for service and shaping them into a long-range, strategic plan for service and technology

This method, used successfully by the authors in real-world situations, is designed to carry out the above in a relatively brief period of time, minimizing the process's impact on people's time and work schedules.

The entire process can be completed in two days. This means that the planning group members should function in a joint, collaborative mode throughout most of the proceedings, that is, there should be no small group or break-out sessions. However, in the interest of ensuring responses to the unique needs of, say, different libraries or groups, it may be necessary to conduct parts of the process separately. In general, the participants should be encouraged to work quickly and efficiently in order to complete in a short time what often requires weeks to accomplish.

USING A FACILITATOR TO PLAN

Try to use a neutral party—a knowledgeable outside person not directly involved with your library—to facilitate the planning process. This allows the planning participants to relate to that person unencumbered by history or reporting relationships. It also ensures that no one associated with the library ends up excluded from being a participant because of having to lead the process.

The planning process proposed here emphasizes collaboration that is intended to generate ideas. Once thoughts have been freely expressed through brainstorming, they are prioritized, then shaped into a strategic vision encompassing a mission, goals, objectives, and actions. The process itself is the vehicle by which the final plan is created, which guarantees that the plan's conception, language, and spirit are those of the planning participants, not those of the facilitator or consultant. In its final form, the plan will be a consensus document, forged through an interactive give-and-take.

STEP ONE: IDENTIFYING THE PLANNING PARTICIPANTS

There are no hard-and-fast rules here except to make sure that you include representation from all those who have a stake in the outcome of your automation efforts. Invite individuals from the different departments of your library as well as lay persons from your community or clientele. If you are automating in cooperation with another library or libraries, the planning process should be collaborative from the start, and the group of participants should reflect the nature of the project.

The total number of participants should not exceed 25. If you have much beyond that number, the process will become unwieldy and is likely to bog down. Do not exclude important constituencies, but keep the size of the planning group manageable. It is better to schedule a second planning session than to carry on with an unmanageable number.

STEP TWO: CONDUCTING BRAINSTORMING EXERCISES

Following introductions and the obligatory logistical announcements, the planning facilitator should begin with some basic ground rules that will foster collaboration and creativity. The handouts shown here as Figures 5–1 and 5–2 are examples that make important points but that do so in an easygoing, nonthreatening fashion. These will break the ice and allow the facilitator to defuse tension in an acceptable manner as the process moves forward.

EXERCISE 1

With the preliminaries out of the way, the brainstorming can begin. In round-robin fashion, the facilitator will ask meeting participants to identify what are referred to in strategic planning parlance as "SWOTs". These are Strengths, Weaknesses, Opportunities, and Threats that exist in the library's operating environment and are likely to impact on the outcome of any planning effort. Examples, some of which may fit more than one category, include:

> hard-working staff that is unafraid of change
> staff that is averse to expanding the use of technology
> declining municipal budget
> clientele that is technologically literate (or illiterate)
> board/council/CEO committed to strengthening library and information services
> rapidly changing user population (demographically-speaking)
> weakening local economy

EXERCISE 2

Later, in similar round-robin style, the facilitator should engage the participants in a second brainstorming exercise to elicit their visions, perceptions, and needs pertaining to library services and technology. This can be done by posing the following question:

> "What do you think should be the priorities for service in (*name of library, consortium, media center*) in the first decade of the twenty-first century?"

Figure 5–1 Technology Planning Project Handout: Rules of the Road

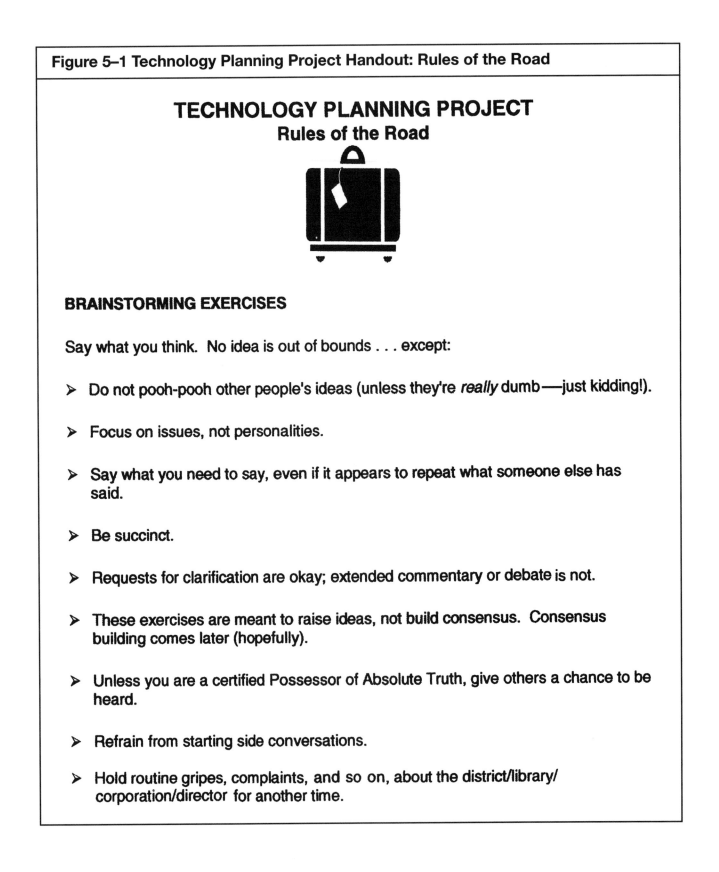

TECHNOLOGY PLANNING PROJECT
Rules of the Road

BRAINSTORMING EXERCISES

Say what you think. No idea is out of bounds . . . except:

➢ Do not pooh-pooh other people's ideas (unless they're *really* dumb—just kidding!).

➢ Focus on issues, not personalities.

➢ Say what you need to say, even if it appears to repeat what someone else has said.

➢ Be succinct.

➢ Requests for clarification are okay; extended commentary or debate is not.

➢ These exercises are meant to raise ideas, not build consensus. Consensus building comes later (hopefully).

➢ Unless you are a certified Possessor of Absolute Truth, give others a chance to be heard.

➢ Refrain from starting side conversations.

➢ Hold routine gripes, complaints, and so on, about the district/library/ corporation/director for another time.

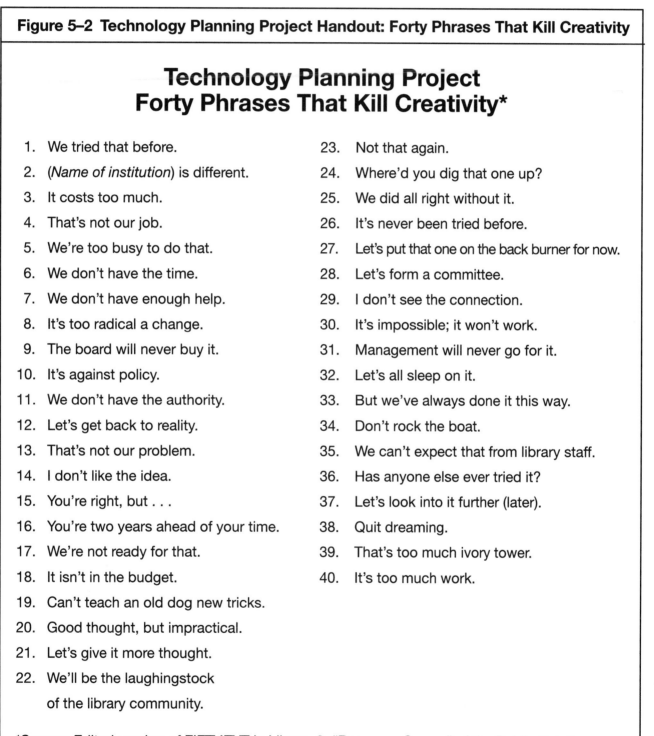

Figure 5–2 Technology Planning Project Handout: Forty Phrases That Kill Creativity

Technology Planning Project
Forty Phrases That Kill Creativity*

1. We tried that before.
2. (*Name of institution*) is different.
3. It costs too much.
4. That's not our job.
5. We're too busy to do that.
6. We don't have the time.
7. We don't have enough help.
8. It's too radical a change.
9. The board will never buy it.
10. It's against policy.
11. We don't have the authority.
12. Let's get back to reality.
13. That's not our problem.
14. I don't like the idea.
15. You're right, but . . .
16. You're two years ahead of your time.
17. We're not ready for that.
18. It isn't in the budget.
19. Can't teach an old dog new tricks.
20. Good thought, but impractical.
21. Let's give it more thought.
22. We'll be the laughingstock of the library community.

23. Not that again.
24. Where'd you dig that one up?
25. We did all right without it.
26. It's never been tried before.
27. Let's put that one on the back burner for now.
28. Let's form a committee.
29. I don't see the connection.
30. It's impossible; it won't work.
31. Management will never go for it.
32. Let's all sleep on it.
33. But we've always done it this way.
34. Don't rock the boat.
35. We can't expect that from library staff.
36. Has anyone else ever tried it?
37. Let's look into it further (later).
38. Quit dreaming.
39. That's too much ivory tower.
40. It's too much work.

*Source: Edited version of FIFTY.TXT in Library 2, "Resource Co-op," of the Public Relations and Marketing Forum, CompuServe.

A METHOD FOR ASSIGNING POINT VALUES

1. Each participant receives the same number of points as there are items—e.g., 50 points for 50 items—and a pack of Post-its.
2. Instruct participants to distribute points as they wish, with their higher priorities getting the greater number of points.
3. Ask participants to assign no more than 10 points to any one item.
4. Instruct participants to write the number of points they are assigning in the center of the Post-it, and the number of the item in the corner (that's in case the Post-it falls off).
5. When everyone has finished attaching the Post-it scores to the respective items, total and write in the number of points received by each item. Use a different color marker for the totals than was used to record the ideas.
6. Create a new chart listing the highest priority items

These ideas are likely to range from the very narrowly focused—"Get our patrons to return their materials on time"—to the more lofty issues—"Give our users 24/7 access to resources around the world."

In both brainstorming exercises, the participants' ideas are listed on newsprint as they are mentioned.

STEP THREE: ASSIGNING POINT VALUES

Participants should then be asked to prioritize both the environmental issues and their "visions" by assigning point values to the ideas that have been articulated by the entire group. Separately prioritize SWOT factors (as a whole and across all four factors) and visioning ideas.

The sidebar above offers a simple method of assigning priority point values, which has the added benefit of getting everyone to move around!

STEP FOUR: ESTABLISHING ISSUES, GOALS, AND OBJECTIVES

Now, shape the SWOT priorities into environmental "issue areas" and the service visions into a statement of purpose, goals, objectives, and actions (refer to Chapter 4 for definitions of these terms). Together, these will constitute the long-range, strategic plan that will help to guide the library's technology efforts.

The environmental issues can either simply be included for "awareness" purposes as part of the document or be a springboard for participants to develop "strategic responses" to them. These are action steps to be taken *in response* to the perceived environmental impact. For example, a perception of "declining resources for library services" might generate a response to "organize a campaign to strengthen governmental or corporate awareness of the value of information." (**Note**: Creating strategic responses to environmental issues will likely stretch this process beyond two days.)

The mission statement/goals/objectives/actions will become the heart of the plan, establishing the basis for future technological and other development. (Here is where you will use the Technology Planning Worksheet offered in Chapter 4.) Given the rapid rate of change, it is probably wise to create a plan that projects no more than three years into the future.

CONCLUSION

It must be emphasized that this is a modified strategic planning process. Its primary purpose is to give people an opportunity to express their concerns and ideas and to work with others to fashion a consensus around some basic principles. Building a fully developed strategic plan is secondary to the interaction and communication that takes place during this process. In other words, what the participants go through is at least as important as the outcome.

Finally, some benefits characterizing the process as a whole include the following:

1. People who have little or no experience with group processes will become familiar with a form of working together

that is becoming more commonplace in this age of "teams" and distributed responsibility.

2. Persons who previously had little contact with one another will have an opportunity to develop a greater understanding for concerns within other areas and departments of the organization or within other organizations and institutions.

3. Participants are encouraged to think and then to express whatever is on their mind in a process relatively free of bureaucratic constraints.

4. Ideas become separated from the persons who expressed them, inhibiting the tendency to associate suggestions, particularly those we do not like, with the person(s) who articulated them.

SOURCES

As noted, the methodology described above has been tested in actual planning situations. Coauthors Ann Kelsey and John M. Cohn have used this approach many times in their independent consulting work as DocuMentors. Dr. Cohn has also used these techniques as part of technology planning at County College of Morris in New Jersey. Many other library planning consultants use similar processes in library organizations throughout the country. Groups of all kinds—staff in local public libraries, representatives from member libraries in single- or multi-type library consortia, campus faculty and staff, information center staff in corporate settings—have all been exposed to this approach for one-, two-, or three-day periods. It works, giving participants a sense of involvement in decision-making, as well as generating useful ideas for technology plans and for the implementation of automated systems.

For additional approaches to the process outlined here, see the following:

Allison, Mike, and Jude Kaye. 1997. *Strategic Planning for Nonprofit Organizations: A Practical Guide and Workbook.* New York: John Wiley.
This book breaks strategic planning into six steps or phases, plus a monitoring and evaluation phase, using worksheets, checklists, and tables, in print and on diskette, and carries a real-life case study through the entire process. "Acknowledging that different organizations have different needs and resources, this . . . guide presents a process that can be adjusted to work for a 1- to 2-day planning retreat or for a longer, 6- to 12-month planning

cycle." The book targets mainly small- and medium-sized nonprofit organizations of all kinds.

"Free Management Library's On-Line Nonprofit Organization Development Program Module #6: Developing Your Strategic Plan." Revised October 5, 2000 [Online]. Available: www.managementhelp.org/np_progs/sp_mod/str_plan.htm [2001, February 26].
This site is part of the Free Management Library(SM), a "complete, highly integrated library for nonprofits and for-profits," developed by Carter McNamara, Authenticity Consulting, LLC. The site includes a link to a *Framework for a Basic Nonprofit Strategic Plan Document* that allows you to write a draft of your own strategic plan by filling in the form as you proceed through the various activities described. There is also a link to a section entitled *How Many Planning Meetings Will We Need?* that includes "An Example Planning Process and Design of Meetings."

6 A PLANNING APPROACH FOR EVALUATING AND AMENDING YOUR TECHNOLOGY PLAN

WHY ARE ASSESSMENT AND EVALUATION IMPORTANT?

At the same time that new technologies are creating opportunities for improved and innovative services, public institutions—as well as corporate—are under increasing pressure to demonstrate their accountability and productivity. "How do we know that all this money that we're spending on_____(fill in the blank) is accomplishing anything?" "Can you demonstrate that there have been improvements in _____(again, fill in the blank) by virtue of our having committed all those dollars to expensive technologies?" What this means is that a library's continuing success will depend in part on its ability to identify and *communicate* the contributions technologies have made to its program.

In terms of a library's technology, accountability means measuring and evaluating the effectiveness of the plan in carrying forward the library's stated goals. This is important to do because certain outcomes may be dependent upon your doing so. Outcomes include, among others:

- maintaining stakeholder support for your technology-based initiatives
- redefining constituency needs and expectations based upon what you learn
- ensuring that governing authorities will continue to fund your program
- establishing sufficient credibility so that your future initiatives will be well received
- having confidence that the technologies you have adopted are really helping you to meet your service objectives

- learning from your initial experiences so that you can shape future plans more effectively

INCORPORATING ASSESSMENT AND EVALUATION IN TECHNOLOGY PLANS: SOME EXAMPLES

More and more libraries, or their parent institutions, are incorporating assessment into their technology plans. It is often a requirement. Here are some examples:

➢ As noted in Chapter 4, many libraries are benefiting from the Universal Service ("*e-rate*") program of telecommunications discounts. To qualify, libraries must submit a technology plan that includes an evaluation component. The Texas State Library recommends that libraries address the following questions in their plans:

EVALUATION PROCESS:

1. How will this library evaluate the success of this plan?
2. How will you determine if the technology plan was successful in meeting the goals of your institutional plans?
3. How frequently will you update the plan?

Source: *Technology Plan in Support of E-Rate.*
July 20, 2000 [Online]. Available:
www.tsl.state.tx.us/ld/funding/techplan.html
[2001, March 2].

➤ Schools and school districts have long incorporated assessment methodologies as part of their planning process. The following is an example of evaluation requirements in a New Jersey district's technology plan:

IV. Evaluation Plan—Computer Technology Advisory Council will be responsible for monitoring and assessing the progress of the Technology Plan. The committee will:

A. Meet at least three times a school year . . . to assess the implementation of the Technology Plan.

B. Assess the progress of staff development with regard to support staff, faculty, administration, and student computer literacy.

C. Assess the degree to which technology has been integrated into normal classroom teaching.

D. Assess the degree to which technology has enhanced communication between the school and the community.

E. Assess the district's progress toward . . . maintaining an updated district-wide technology plan.

F. Submit an annual evaluation report to the superintendent's cabinet.

Source: *Morris Hills Regional District Plan for Technology 1997–2002.* Updated April 2000 [Online]. Available: www.mhrd.k12.nj.us/mhhs/techplan/default.htm [2001, March 2].

➤ Lastly, to Kansas City, Kansas, Community College (KCKCC) the purpose of technology plan evaluation is to develop "an ongoing model for technology use . . . and to improve technology implementation and use throughout the campus and the community." The sidebar on the following page contains a partial list of what Kansas City, Kansas, Community College sees evaluation accomplishing.

THE EVALUATION WILL:

- be a continuous process for effective decision making and will include everyone associated with the use of technology at KCKCC
- put students, teachers, and community partners at the heart of assessment
- be used to help facilitate the effectiveness of the technology use at KCKCC
- assess the process of the implementation of technology at KCKCC
- be useful to support learning of what is working and where changes might need to be made in the Technology Plan

Source: *Kansas City Kansas Community College Technology Plan, 1997-98.*
May 12, 1999 [Online]. Available: www.kckcc.cc.ks.us/it/ techplan.htm#eval [2001, March 2].

GETTING INPUT ON WHAT YOU HAVE ACCOMPLISHED WITH TECHNOLOGY

There are many ways to accomplish assessment and evaluation. Some of them may be dictated by a governing body or parent institution. Approaches are suggested by the sidebar examples above. In this book, we have placed considerable importance on gauging the perceptions of your stakeholders. Accordingly, we propose an exercise that is a step toward helping you to evaluate your technology plan and what it has (or has not) accomplished.

Following the methodology described in the previous chapter, you can use a brainstorming or discussion exercise to encourage a new round of planning participants to look back over the period covered by your technology plan. This will serve as the basis for looking ahead to the time period that will be covered by your next plan and give participants the opportunity to think about how the library can best implement or enhance technology to meet people's needs.

Using the worksheet represented by Figure 6–1, and having been encouraged to fill it out in advance of the day of planning, participants will be asked to:

Figure 6–1 A Planning Worksheet for Assessing Your Technology Plan

Strategy	Strengths	Weaknesses	Modifications That Would Improve	Summary Evaluation
				❑ Maintain ❑ Replace with a new or revised strategy ❑ Terminate
				❑ Maintain ❑ Replace with a new or revised strategy ❑ Terminate
				❑ Maintain ❑ Replace with a new or revised strategy ❑ Terminate
				❑ Maintain ❑ Replace with a new or revised strategy ❑ Terminate
				❑ Maintain ❑ Replace with a new or revised strategy ❑ Terminate

Source: This worksheet is based on one in *Creating and Implementing Your Strategic Plan: A Workbook for Public and Nonprofit Organizations*, by John M. Bryson and Farnum K. Alston (San Francisco: Jossey-Bass, 1996, p. 107).

- identify existing technology-based initiatives—these are what the term "strategy" refers to in the worksheet
- evaluate these initiatives
- suggest alternative, new, or modified approaches in the context of services that already exist

The planning goal will be to establish a consensus on proposed continuing and new technology initiatives and to prioritize them.

USING YOUR PLAN IN NEW AND CREATIVE WAYS

Doing an assessment and evaluation of your technology plan will also give you the opportunity to think of other, ancillary ways of using your plan. These may not relate directly to guiding expenditures or enabling a particular service. However, they may allow you to get even more mileage out of the plan you worked hard to create. For example:

- Use your plan as a vehicle for publicizing the library and its services. Turn it into a brochure or news piece, making it possible for you to focus your clientele's attention on a major activity with important implications for service. Emphasize how the plan came about with the participation of the library's users as well as its staff.
- Share your plan with other agencies, departments, or colleagues that are not part of your stakeholder group. Others will learn more about the library and will (or *should*) be impressed with the fact that you are a planner. You may even get some useful ideas from others who use technology in ways similar to how you use it in your library.
- Use the plan to seek out grant opportunities from state and regional sources and little-known or newly created grant opportunities from national, state, and local foundations that give money to libraries. A well-developed plan of any kind is a requirement for most grant-funding sources. You will be a huge step ahead as you explore such possibilities or as you find out about such opportunities (usually two weeks prior to a deadline—much too late to "throw a plan together"). State library agencies often make grants to encourage consortial membership, and sometimes a compo-

nent of your plan that is particularly "cutting edge" may be eligible for a special grant designed to encourage innovation and to promote pilot projects and new services.

- Use your plan to open discussions with comparable organizations such as museums to see if you have needs in common that would allow you to form what has become known as a "strategic alliance." Essentially, newly opened dialogues give organizations the opportunity to pursue goals in a collaborative fashion, to the benefit of all parties.

- Share your plan and its vision with new staff members as one way of having them learn about the library once they are "on board." For some, it will be an opportunity to grasp the broader picture, while for others, it may spark interests that could propel them to become valuable participants in future planning endeavors.

These are just a sampling of ideas. You can probably come up with others. The point is to use your technology plan to its best advantage in promoting your library and strengthening its mission.

SOURCES

Appleton Public Library. *Technology Plan 1999–2002.* June 14, 1999 [Online]. Available: www.apl.org/policies/tecplan.html [2001, March 2].
The section on evaluation is brief but does show how assessment relates to the rest of the planning document in a public library environment.

Arkansas School District Technology Planning Committee. *Arkansas K–12 School District's Electronic School District Technology Planning Guide.* 1998 [Online]. Available: http://arkedu.state.ar.us/ade-guide/index.html [2001, March 2].
This Web site presents the school district's detailed "road map" that will enable the district to develop a technology plan that meets the requirements set forth in various state and federal grant programs. This page provides links to the many other pages that are part of the electronic planning guide, including "Evaluating a Technology Plan—Basics" [. . . /ade-guide/eval_ techb.html], "Evaluation of the Technology Plan—Indicators" [. . . ade-guide/tp_indicate.html], and "Evaluating the Implementation of a Technology Plan" [. . . /ade-guide/eval_impl.html].

North Central Regional Technology in Education Consortium. *Guiding Questions for Technology Planning*. 2001 [Online]. Available: www.ncrtec.org/capacity/guidewww/gqhome.htm [2001, February 17].

This site discusses basic principles of technology planning, the relationship of technology to your "vision of learning," the "supportive infrastructure" of a plan (training, development, and support), and, in particular for this chapter, "Evaluating the Implementation of Your Technology Plan" [. . . / guide/eval.htm].

PART II:
SELECTING AND IMPLEMENTING INTEGRATED LIBRARY SYSTEMS

There are a number of different paths to system implementation available to libraries. Over the years, the options have changed. For example, at one time, some institutions had data-processing staff that wanted to write software for a custom-made system designed to run on equipment already available on-site. The complexity of library operations, the prohibitive cost of this option in person-hours, time, and computing resources, and today's emphasis on local systems as portals in a global environment have eliminated this option.

Similarly, libraries in the 1960s, '70s, and '80s often bought large mainframe-based or more affordable minicomputer-based systems with accompanying proprietary library application software. Today, mainframe- and minicomputer-based systems still exist, but are often considered "legacy," or outdated, products by libraries and vendors alike.

Your challenge will be to identify options that are available for implementing a library system, then assessing their benefits to your library. You must consider these options in relation to (1) the priorities that emerged out of your library profile and strategic planning, (2) the nature and quality of the alternatives that are available to you, and (3) the cost of these alternatives.

Chapters 7 and 8 will review how integrated systems have evolved and what options are available to libraries for deciding on how to implement a system. Chapter 9 begins with a *System Implementation Checklist* that outlines a basic seven-phased process that is applicable to all libraries. The steps in the Checklist are covered in detail in Chapter 9 and the subsequent chapters of Part II.

7 THE "NEW" INTEGRATED SYSTEMS: USER EXPECTATIONS AND SYSTEM CAPABILITIES

HOW HAS THE INTEGRATED SYSTEMS ENVIRONMENT CHANGED?

For many libraries, the most important materials accessible through their local system are the library's own, in-house collection of books and audiovisual holdings. However, as we know, Web sites, virtual collections, e-journals, digitized historical records, full-motion video, electronic academic reserves, and many other resources made possible by new technologies, are today part of a library's collection as well. Indeed, the concept of systems as "local" is disappearing as library networks become nodes in cyberspace—sites among many other sites on the amorphous Internet. Accordingly, electronic and virtual collections must be made as accessible through your automated system as are the books and CDs on your shelves.

Chapter 1 referred to new, more powerful system functionality that is driving libraries to migrate from older automated systems to newer ones. This chapter will discuss in more detail how the newer generations of integrated systems enable libraries to meet their users' diverse and expanding information expectations.

THE EVOLVING INFORMATION ENVIRONMENT: WHAT THE USER EXPECTS

User needs vary, hence the need for careful planning and stakeholder involvement in the planning process. However, we can discern some overall trends that are increasingly characteristic of the expectations of library clientele today—in all types of libraries:

- The general use and acceptance of the World Wide Web and standard browsers are leading users to expect the same kind of access in online library catalogs.
- Users expect not merely a seamless integration of resources but a common, graphical interface through which they access these resources.
- Users expect quick if not instantaneous response times to complex queries across a myriad of databases.
- Users expect all varieties of formats of information to be available to them.
- Users want to be able to access the same resources they can get in the library from remote locations such as their homes and offices.
- Users expect to be able to access the library's resources 24 hours a day, 7 days a week.
- Users may expect electronic assistance or mediation to replace or supplement human interaction.
- Users prefer systems that allow maximum opportunity for "self-service" features and user-initiated manipulation of the system. This includes, for example, the ability to place an interlibrary loan request, reserve a book, create lists of materials in different formats for research purposes, or to interactively exchange information with library staff or other users of the library system.
- Users want personalization and customization of services, including personal profiles and preferences, topical alerts, and the ability to save past search results for ongoing reference.

THE EVOLVING INFORMATION ENVIRONMENT: WHAT IT MEANS FOR LIBRARY SYSTEMS

What impact do these user expectations have in relation to today's library systems? Throughout this book, we use the phrase "*integrated* library system." Some think "integrated" implies completeness—that today's systems offer everything that a library needs to automate its functions and services. In fact, the term really means to coordinate or blend into a functioning whole.

In developing specifications for acquiring a system, libraries must consider not only how systems handle fund accounting, the cataloging of a book, or the circulation of audiovisual materials. They must consider how well the system coordinates access to the vast array of resources and formats available today. Here are some specific points, in no particular order:

- Systems must be able to provide and manage access to resources in many different print, digital, and audiovisual formats sited both within a given library and in remote locations such as other libraries and the Internet.
- Systems must serve not only as gateways to remote resources, but they must be able to organize the access to all resources in a smooth, seamless fashion.
- Systems must accommodate the increasing variety of formats in which information is found and be able to adhere to the emerging standards developed for these formats.
- Systems must employ interfaces that are graphical and browser-like, with search options that are powerful yet customizable to the various levels of user expertise.
- Systems must be able to support the resource-sharing, document-exchange, and database-licensing practices that are standard within consortia and among individual libraries.
- Systems must extend the ability of the end user to manipulate both information content and the system's functionality, for example, create personalized bibliographies and links to other resources, place an interlibrary loan, or legally download materials from many locations.
- Systems must provide individualized services based on users' profiles and preferences, such as new materials alerts and the dissemination of selected information (SDI) based on the users profile and topical interests.

- Systems must enable user access to the system from remote locations such as home or office in support of both "reference" inquiries and the more sustained use associated with distance education courses.
- Systems must be able to interface the library with other systems in related or parent organizations such as municipal governments, corporate headquarters, school districts, or academic computing centers.
- Systems must support the library as a knowledge distributor and *producer* and by incorporating recordkeeping and management capabilities related to publishing, copyright, and intellectual property concerns.
- Systems must provide flexible, customized statistical information and management reports to allow ongoing evaluation of the systems' usage and the library's resource allocation decisions.

EXPANDING SYSTEM POTENTIAL: SOME EXAMPLES

Figure 7–1 offers some examples of how vendors of integrated library systems are adding functionality that expands the library's ability to take advantage of the Internet and new technologies. These examples are offered as illustrative of how the system vendors are responding to the changing information environment.

It is clear that these changes are impacting all kinds of systems. The Follett Corporation, for example, targets the education market and libraries in K–12 schools. Ex Libris, on the other hand, develops systems that are geared to large research libraries and consortia. These and other system vendors have one thing in common: They must all enable their library customers to offer library users a "one-stop shopping" approach to information organization and retrieval that maximizes the potential of today's technologies. By the time this book is published, system capabilities will have expanded even more to keep up with the rapid pace of technological change.

In the chapters that follow, newer system capabilities are considered alongside libraries' more traditional concerns in the context of developing comprehensive specifications for system comparison and procurement. Today's library is both a physical place and a virtual environment, really many libraries at once in a global setting. To the user, boundaries are falling and transparency is the name of the game. Integrated systems, as they coordinate and blend, must reflect this new reality of library service.

Figure 7–1 Beyond Traditional Automation: A Sampling of Services

LIBRARY SYSTEM VENDOR	PARTNER or INTEGRATED APPLICATION	CONTENT / PRODUCT / SERVICE
epixtech *www.epixtech.com/products/ilibrary.asp*	In development	*ilibrary* will connect users with integrated library systems, databases, community information resources, and Internet information, such as e-mail and top news stories.
Ex Libris *www.exlibris-usa.com*	MetaLib *www.exlibris-usa.com*	*MetaLib* and its *SFX* software provide libraries with a customizable user interface for retrieving, linking to, organizing, and using scholarly information from different library catalogs and electronic databases.
Follett Software Company *www.fsc.follett.com*	Webivore Knowledge Systems *www.webivore.com*	Through the *WebPath Express* Subscription Service, MARC 856 electronic access tags are integrated directly into the library's Follett system database, providing OPAC users with links to thousands of Internet sites.
Innovative Interfaces, Inc. *www.iii.com*	netLibrary, Inc. *www.netLibrary.com*	Users of the INNOPAC catalog in Innovative's Millennium system have full-text access to netLibrary's e-books through full MARC records that are downloaded into the library's catalog.
SIRSI Corporation *www.sirsi.com*	InfoBistro.com *www.infobistro.com*	Through InfoBistro (or *iBistro*), a customized Internet "e-library" portal, users of SIRSI's WebCat online catalog (or other non-SIRSI system catalog) can access enhanced information about the materials held by the library, including cover images, tables of contents, abstracts, and book reviews.
The Library Corporation (TLC) *www.tlcdelivers.com/tlc/solution/mainysm.htm*	RatingZone *www.ratingzone.com/main/default.asp*	Billed as a "customizable library supersite" TLC's *YouSeeMore* offers an OPAC, news and weather, hot title and bestseller lists, ready reference, and the library's calendar of events. It includes the *RatingZone*, a Web service that recommends books, movies, and music, and predicts which items patrons will enjoy based upon their own ratings.

All sites accessed between February and April 2001.

SOURCES

Barber, David. 2000. "Internet-Accessible Full-Text Electronic Journal & Periodical Collections for Libraries." *Library Technology Reports* 36, no. 5 (September-October): 112.
The first section focuses on the user's experiences with the Web sites that provide access to full-text periodical databases and journal archives. The second section addresses the internal library operations that must occur before those users can gain access to those Web sites, including the selection of providers and licensing strategies. The third section contains a directory of journal aggregators and periodical database publishers.

Barry, Jeff. 2001. "Closing in on Content." *Library Journal* 126, no. 6 (April 1): 46–58. (This is *LJ*'s "Automated System Marketplace" article for the year 2001.)
The "Marketplace" is an annual feature that offers valuable information comparing vendor and system sales and numbers of sites by type of library. The article for 2001 includes a discussion of "content providers entering the systems arena," referring to the availability of such Amazon.com-like features as book reviews and linkages to other sources through integrated library systems. See references to this and the preceding year's article in the Sources for Chapter 10.

Breeding, Marshall. 2000. "ALA Conference 2000." *Information Today* 17, no. 8 (September 1): 60–61.
"In the current library automation market . . . (t)he main battleground of competition that differentiates one competitor from another now lies in the products and services that operate beyond the traditional scope of library automation. Each vendor now seeks to deliver new and better ways to help libraries provide a more comprehensive and integrated environment of information resources." Conference roundup articles of this type are an excellent source of information on changes among the system vendors as well as on new product developments.

Ex Libris. "MetaLib Overview." No date [Online]. Available: www.exlibris-usa.com/metalib/overview.html [2001, February 16].
This is one of several sites within the Ex Libris home page that describe the MetaLib interface and its underlying application technologies that are marketed as part of Ex Libris' Aleph 500 integrated system. Although the system is intended for very large libraries and consortia, readers from all types of libraries may wish to refer to this site for its description of how one library systems vendor conceptualizes the integrating of diverse sources and formats of information within an automated library system.

Harley, Bruce. 1999. "Electronic One-Stop Shopping: The Good, the Bad, and the Ugly." *Information Technology and Libraries* 18, no. 4 (December): 200–209.

"One-stop shopping has been the operational theme for electronic information services offered by the San Diego State University Library since 1994 . . . This article explores not just the good, but the bad and the ugly of the library's one-stop shopping approach to the delivery of electronic information." Topics include making as many electronic resources as possible accessible remotely, providing access to multiple databases, and using the Web as a uniform database interface.

Pearce, Judith, et. al. "The Challenge of Integrated Access: The Hybrid Library System of the Future." June 2, 2000 [Online]. Available: www.nla.gov.au/nla/staffpaper/jpearce1.html [2001, March 24].
This paper, prepared by staff members of the National Library of Australia, presents an analysis of the concept of the modern "hybrid" information environment. This environment is described as "one where an appropriate range of heterogeneous information services is presented to the user in a consistent and integrated way via a single interface. It may include local and/or remote distributed services, both print and electronic." The article analyzes the different levels of "integrated access" that are possible and reviews how "integrated" library systems must change to support a wider array of materials and objects as well as service capabilities. It contains a useful bibliography of related sources.

Reade, Tripp. 2001. "Unpacking the Trunk: Customization and MyLibrary@ NCState." *Computers in Libraries* 21, no.2 (February): 29–34.
This article describes North Carolina State's *MyLibrary*, a Web page that allows users to identify interests by topic and by type of material (new titles, electronic journals, library links, indexes and abstracts, messages from my librarian, and so on). The resulting service provides users with updated information of particular interest to them each time they log on to the system. Guest access to the service is available at http://my.lib.ncsu.edu.

Rogers, Eric. 2000. "Designing a Web-Based Desktop That's Easy to Navigate." *Computers in Libraries* 20, no. 4 (April): 34–40.
This article focuses on the process of planning and developing a Web-based computer desktop at Kansas City Public Library. The reason for this activity included, among others, "a long-term goal of developing a unified interface to a variety of electronic library resources."

Stielow, Frederick, ed. 1999. *Creating a Virtual Library: A How-To-Do-It Manual* (Number 91). New York: Neal-Schuman.
This book is a guide for the planning, setting up, and maintaining of a virtual library, by which the authors mean that "all services are provided through the Internet, rather than in a building." Although the book does not deal with integrated library systems per se, its focus on ensuring that "the special qualities of (the) physical library are translated into cyberspace" is one important factor in the library's evaluation of system options and products.

3 IDENTIFYING OPTIONS FOR IMPLEMENTING AN INTEGRATED SYSTEM

While the focus of this book is on a library acquiring its own integrated system, there are variations on and alternatives to this model. The principles for planning, for turning priorities into system specifications, and for evaluating systems, however, are the same or comparable across the various options. These options are presented below.

WHAT INTEGRATED SYSTEM OPTIONS ARE AVAILABLE TO LIBRARIES?

Options include:

- *Acquire software and hardware or acquire software to run on a computer network already in place.* Until the 1990s, acquiring an integrated system usually meant buying what the library system vendors referred to as *turnkey* systems. "Turnkey" meant commercially available, off-the-shelf systems that housed complete hardware and software configurations for library purposes. Today, the majority of library software packages are designed to run on local or wide area networks that utilize powerful microcomputer servers and personal computer workstations. In these instances, if the appropriate hardware, operating system software, and network architecture are already in place, a library may use its available network to run a library system application. If hardware needs to be upgraded or replaced, the library may obtain more favorable prices by using a computer manufacturer or wholesaler rather than the library system vendor.
- *Join with another library or several libraries to buy a new system.* It may be desirable to join with others to purchase a system as an alternative to acquiring a "stand-alone" system. There are often advantages to joint planning and working with others to implement major technological initiatives

in your library. However, two do not necessarily live as cheaply as one, so that buying a larger system with more equipment, storage, memory, and so forth might in fact cost substantially more money, depending on the particular situation. Moreover, in planning, it is important to consider the presence, or absence, of shared goals and objectives, of a history of cooperation and collaboration, among the participating institutions.

The library is often part of a larger organization or corporation—as in the case of a campus library, individual school library within a district, or corporate division or branch library. In such instances, joint planning and purchase are probably worth the additional work involved in the interest of promoting the overall organizational mission and service goals.

- *Join an existing integrated system or consortium of libraries.* Many libraries do not acquire their own system, whether alone or with other libraries, but instead elect to join with an already existing network of libraries or with consortia that offer integrated system participation as a membership option. The decision to join something that already exists may stem from such considerations as cost, local politics, convenience, the availability or lack of staff with technical skills, or a combination of these.

  Consortium participation often provides significant cost savings, particularly in terms of systems staff, and membership in a larger system may make more sophisticated services easier to acquire and introduce. On the down side, decisions regarding new features and services will be made by committee, limiting the individual library's ability to control its own destiny.

  Currently, approximately 10 percent of libraries acquiring new systems do so as consortium members, and while specific data is not available, statistics by library type suggest that this figure may be closer to one-third of all public and college and university libraries purchasing or upgrading systems. For school and special libraries, this figure is much lower.

- *Contract to purchase a system operated by the vendor.* Known as the "application service provider" model, this option is a relatively new one in the world of libraries. It involves the vendors hosting and supporting their own products. Essentially, the library customer gets access to integrated system functionality via the Internet and pays the vendor both for this access and for services provided. The end-user organization—your library—does not have to install software, maintain equipment, or worry about attracting and retaining technical staff to run a system. This option will be discussed further below.

Measuring the above options against your library profile and the goals and objectives of your strategic plan will likely result in the elimination of one or more alternatives. How best to evaluate the remaining options? Some possibilities include:

- Read about system options in journal articles and in reviews such as those in *Library Technology Reports.*
- Visit libraries that have implemented the options that interest you.
- Attend conferences at which library system vendors will discuss their systems and provide demonstrations of them.
- Hire a consultant to assist you in evaluating each option and to work with you in determining what is appropriate for your library. (See Appendix: Working with Consultants.)

UNDERSTANDING THE NETWORKED ENVIRONMENT

Regardless of the option you select, it is important to understand that all systems today are part of a networked environment. In the past, only libraries with branches or those linked to a consortium worried about building a network. This has changed, however, as library systems have become more graphical, more integrated with global Web-based resources, and more accessible to users from their desktops wherever those desktops might be. Now, *all libraries, not just consortia and libraries with remote sites, must plan network environments for their systems.* Because of that, we present a "tutorial" on what it means for a system to be part of a network.

INTRODUCTION

The simple connections of years gone by that joined dumb terminals to a host computer are rapidly being replaced in libraries by local area networks (LANs) that allow users working on PCs to view information in a graphical environment. With the ascension of the World Wide Web as a means of access to global information resources, automated library systems operating on LANs are becoming more common, displacing the older (legacy) systems running on host mainframes, minicomputers, or super-microcomputers. Many of these new systems are employing client/server architecture in which a *client* requests services and a *server* computer provides them. Unlike the hierarchical computer(host)/dumb terminal (slave) model, a given computer may function as both client and server, may connect to multiple servers and clients simultaneously, and may operate on different computer platforms.

The distribution of tasks among clients and servers is handled in a variety of different ways. Some systems may retain the bulk of the activity on the server, with the client workstations assuming only a small part of the processing responsibility. Systems that rely primarily on the server also include the new "thin client" networks, in which individual client workstations have minimal storage and RAM (no hard drives) and a single copy of the software resides on the server. Other systems may distribute the workload so that the workstations take on more of the processing responsibility. When this happens, the distinction between the server and the workstation becomes blurred. Most of today's integrated systems employ one or a combination of these client/ server models or are in the process of migrating their older systems to such an environment.

LOCAL AREA NETWORKS

A result of this trend is that library system vendors are no longer supplying the peripheral hardware and the telecommunications equipment and cabling needed to run their systems, even when the library is self-contained at a single site. The creation of the network architecture and the telecommunications connections are now becoming the library's or the consortium's responsibility, and the customer is often encouraged to purchase this equipment locally, that is, not from the library systems vendor.

The first step, then, in planning a networked environment for an integrated library system, is to create a *local area network*. This can be done before a library system has been selected, but it must adhere to cabling and networking standards (see Chapter 17) so that most vendors' library systems will run on it. For the majority of integrated library systems—as well as for other applications—this local area network will need to have:

- as many network-ready personal computers with as much storage, speed, cache, and random access memory as the budget allows
- Ethernet network architecture
- Category 5 unshielded twisted pair (UTP) cable supporting data transmission rates (bandwidth) of up to 100 megabytes per second
- Routers, switches, and firewalls
- UNIX/LINUX or Windows NT/2000 network operating system

WIDE AREA NETWORKS

Once you have installed a LAN, it can be extended or connected to other networks in a remote environment by using longer cable runs, if the distance is short, or by using an outside telecommunications provider, if the distance is greater.

When LANs in remote locations are connected together, they become *wide area* or *metropolitan* networks, the best known of which is the Internet. These networks require higher speed lines with greater bandwidth because more data is passing through them over a greater distance.

Telecommunications options commonly used for these networks include:

- T1/frame relay
- integrated services digital network (ISDN)
- asynchronous transfer mode (ATM)

These traditional choices for network connectivity have been joined recently by some new kids on the block, still somewhat young and unproven, but worth watching as possible alternatives for high speed access:

- cable modem
- digital subscriber line (DSL)
- wireless (LAN or WAN)

In order to select the most appropriate telecommunications option that will offer a full range of information services to users at optimum speeds, all libraries must compare competing broadband network service choices carefully, paying particular attention to:

- local availability

- price
- minimum bandwidth and speed guarantees

CONCLUSION

Every library, regardless of size or location, must address these issues in order to connect to the Internet and access the brave new world of Web-based public catalogs and external databases containing text, images, and full-motion video. This access is the payoff for the effective design and implementation of networked systems. Careful planning when initially installing local area and wide area networks, and adherence by both library and vendor to specified standards, ensures reliable, fast access to local and global networked resources for both libraries and users.

JOINING A CONSORTIUM: A SUMMARY OF THE ISSUES

Libraries react to joining a consortium in many ways, depending on a host of factors—only one of which is cost. For example, some libraries may have had a negative experience in a previous consortium. Others may lack a tradition of cooperation or may have a strong history of independent action and decision making. In such instances, a cooperative approach to system implementation is probably not an option, regardless of cost considerations.

Typically, however, cost considerations loom large in the planning process, and a library must carefully identify the costs associated with any technology option. Indeed, for a smaller library, implementing a system may seem overwhelming and out of reach because of the costs involved. For this reason, many libraries seek to automate jointly with other libraries or to become part of an existing system.

The shared expense of togetherness may or may not represent a savings for the individual library. For example, sharing the purchase of a large, complex network that accommodates a great number of users may mean that an individual library's costs will be greater than if the library were to purchase a system independently. Similarly, joining an existing system may cost as much as purchasing a system locally because the system is likely to pass along the costs of adding a new member to the joining library.

Bear in mind, though, that a library's mix of collection size, user base, and activity levels may require that it acquire hardware that, in terms of initial cost, may exceed the costs of a joint venture. Plus, when you add indirect costs (such as staff time) to direct costs (such as purchase price and ongoing expenses), a cooperative approach often proves more cost effective than going it alone.

Consortium participation often provides significant cost savings because a local system operator is not required, and membership in a larger system can provide access to more sophisticated services because consortium staff are able to test and introduce new products for the individual library. Consortia may also be partially supported through state and federal funds as part of a statewide resource-sharing plan, resulting in reduced costs to individual libraries. On the downside, decisions regarding new features and services will be made by committee, limiting the individual library's ability to make changes.

Other benefits to consortium membership include expedited access to the collections of other participating member libraries and the sharing of experience and expertise and the ability to afford a system with capabilities that a single library could not afford.

Currently, approximately 10 percent of libraries acquiring new systems do so as consortium members, and while specific data are not available, statistics by library type suggest that this figure may be closer to one-quarter of all public and college and university libraries purchasing or upgrading systems. Clearly, consortium membership has its attractions to many libraries.

Deciding whether to join a consortium of libraries is complicated and requires a detailed examination of all the elements that are associated with introducing technology into a library operation. In many instances, the library may be best served by first developing its priorities and requirements, then evaluating network membership against these, in effect treating the consortium as if it were a vendor. Because consortium staff are not likely to have the resources to respond to an RFP as a vendor would, a review of consortium membership as an option should be conducted separately, either prior to issuing an RFP or after vendor responses have been evaluated and costs determined. In many states, consortium agreements are exempted from procurement requirements, making this type of two-tiered review possible—and desirable.

USING AN APPLICATION SERVICE PROVIDER

Using an application service provider, or ASP, means making an arrangement whereby vendors host and support their own products, granting the library customer access to integrated system functionality via the Internet. The library does not have to install software, maintain equipment, or worry about attracting and retaining technical staff to run a system.

There are emerging examples of this approach among the library system vendors. For smaller school, special or private collections, **CASPR** offers **LibraryCom**, a service through which library records may be cataloged on or imported into a server maintained by CASPR. These records then become the basis of an online catalog that may be searched by anyone with a standard Web browser. Libraries build and manage their catalog online, paying for the service on the basis of storage and support requirements. (See *www.librarycom.com.*) In similar fashion, **epixtech**, formerly Ameritech Library Services, offers an ASP option with its *Horizon* software. (See *www.epixtech.com.*)

This model is a relatively new one to the library market. While there are examples of libraries using or testing the ASP model, the jury is still out on how widespread adoption will be. Overall, the advantage of ASP is that the library is able to shift responsibility for installing, managing, and maintaining its system to the vendor. On the downside, security remains a concern and the ability the library has to customize its system is still limited.

From a planning perspective, libraries considering this option must do the same kind of planning for a system that they would normally do. The system itself must meet your library's needs, reflect the service priorities you have set, and be affordable—apart from how it is delivered to your library and its users. Still, ASP represents a potentially strong option for libraries of all types and sizes as the complexity of managing networks and systems grows.

SOURCES

Bocher, Bob. "The Advantages and Disadvantages of Sharing an Automated Library System." Wisconsin Department of Library Instruction. Public Library Development. Updated October, 2000 [Online]. Available: www.dpi.state.wi.us/dpi/dltcl/pld/sharing.html [2001, October 11].

This paper defines what a "shared system" is, then goes on to list and discuss the pros and cons of cooperative purchasing and sharing of an automated library system.

Boss, Richard W. 1995. "Facilities Planning for Technology." *Library Technology Reports* 31, no. 4 (July–August): 393–483.
The author considers book storage, workspace planning, and information technology from the perspective of library facilities planning. Of special interest are the sections on automated library systems and on cabling, LANs, and networks that offer useful, nontechnical definitions of networking jargon.

———. 1990. *The Library Manager's Guide to Automation*. 3rd edition. Boston: G.K. Hall.
This book's review of six system procurement options and discussion of the issues involved in costing automated systems remain useful for libraries weighing their system implementation options.

Dzurinko, Mary K. "Application Service Providers." *Integrated Library System Reports*. November, 2000 [Online]. Available: www.ilsr.com/asp.htm [2001, February 3].
This ILSR Report offers an overview of the ASP phenomenon as a form of outsourcing, covering its origins in the business community and its appearance in the integrated library system marketplace. It offers questions to consider in evaluating ASP products and discusses advantages and disadvantages.

Howden, Norman. 1997. *Local Area Networking for the Small Library: A How-To-Do-It Manual for Librarians*. 2d ed. New York: Neal-Schuman.
"Offers clear guidance on every aspect of LAN from start-up through maintenance and trouble shooting." An installation checklist and a user-needs analysis are also included.

Reenstjerna, Fred R. 2001. "Application Service Providers: Can They Solve Libraries' Problems?" *Computers in Libraries* 21, no. 3 (March): 34+.
The author examines the ASP phenomenon, offering a brief history and distinguishing between "enterprise-level" and "consumer-level" ASPs, with examples of consumer-level applications for use in libraries. The article includes a "Webliography for ASPs."

Saffady, William. 2000. "The Status of Library Automation at 2000." *Library Technology Reports* 36, no. 1 (January-February).
This volume reviews the development of automated library services, systems, products, and capabilities from their earliest development to the present. Of particular interest are the sections on integrated library systems, the computing environments for these systems, and related industry trends.

9 TRANSLATING NEEDS AND PRIORITIES INTO SYSTEM SPECIFICATIONS AND A REQUEST FOR PROPOSAL

LIBRARY NEEDS AND PRIORITIES ARE IDENTIFIED: WHAT'S NEXT?

At this point, we turn our attention to taking the library's identified needs and priorities, converting them into specifications for a system procurement process, and developing the RFP—a Request for Proposal. We are assuming that the library is seeking to acquire its own integrated system. However, if the library's preference is to join a consortium with a system already in place, these "specifications" are still important as the basis for determining how well that system will meet its needs.

Figure 9–1—the System Implementation Checklist—outlines a basic seven-phased process that is applicable to all libraries. It is important to understand that the phases outlined, although sequential in some respects, usually overlap and often take place concurrently. For example, preparing your database for conversion should begin *while* you are still exploring options for acquiring a system. Weeding the collection, a process that is an important part of collection development but independent of system selection per se, can have a major impact on the cost of any project involving the library's database. Weeding should be a regular and ongoing part of any library's operations.

Phase 7 is implementing your chosen system. Implementing the system is never really the last phase of the process. From the moment a system is acquired, library staff must evaluate its effectiveness in meeting library service goals and objectives. Systems must be evaluated for possible upgrade or expansion as business increases, functionality is added by the library or by the system vendor, or technologies are improved or enhanced.

DESCRIBING YOUR LIBRARY

You have already documented the processes that occur within the library and how library functions are carried out. For the RFP, you will translate these processes and functions into specifications, that is, what you want your automated system to do, including things that your existing system, whether automated or manual, cannot do. However, you must also describe your library's goals and resources. This is important, because vendors must understand what you hope to accomplish and what kinds of resources you have or will have in order to be able to propose an appropriate system, in terms of functionality and size, for your library.

The following is a list of items to consider when describing your library, with a brief explanation of each item:

- A **narrative profile** will introduce your library in terms of its geographical location, size and scope, parent body or municipality, demographics, interinstitutional relationships, and other elements that will provide background information—a snapshot of who you are and what kind of service program your library offers.
- Your library's **goals and objectives**, particularly as they relate to technology, will inform the vendors of what you expect to accomplish with an integrated library system. This can be accomplished by appending or summarizing your technology plan and pertinent elements of your overall strategic plan.
- A **statistical profile** should include such things as your library's collection size, number of borrowers, transactions (circulation of materials), new acquisitions, and computer workstation count—currently and projected to three years. (More about computer workstations below.) These data are very important because they allow the vendor to "size" and cost-out a system that will meet your needs now and in the foreseeable future. Your projections must not aim too high or too low lest the vendors propose a system for you that is too small to meet your needs or with more capacity than

---

Figure 9–1 A System Implementation Checklist

PHASE 1: SYSTEM IMPLEMENTATION OPTIONS OR ALTERNATIVES AND FINANCIAL PLANNING

Goal: To explore courses of action that the library might take to improve services through an integrated, online system.

Tasks:

1. Examine and outline alternative approaches and possibilities.
2. Define a series of steps for a phased and coordinated plan for automating the library.
3. Identify and evaluate software, hardware, and telecommunications configurations.
4. Determine estimated start-up and ongoing costs of the proposed alternatives and allocate or secure funding for the proposed system.
5. Determine the technical support requirements needed for any proposed plan.

PHASE 2: ANALYSIS OF SHELFLIST OR EXISTING BIBLIOGRAPHIC DATA FILES

Goal: To identify, describe, and document existing shelflist (for first-time system implementation) or machine-readable (for system migration) data files and standardize the data they contain.

Tasks:

1. Institute quality-control measures to assure consistency of entries within the file.
2. Undertake an inventory of the collection.
3. Verify existing bibliographic information in the shelflist or machine-readable records.
4. Locate and add missing bibliographic information to the records.
5. Implement uniform standardized cataloging practices and consistent use of Cutter numbers.

PHASE 3: RETROSPECTIVE CONVERSION (FIRST-TIME IMPLEMENTATION)

Goal: To implement a program of retrospectively converting the library's manual bibliographic database.

Tasks:

1. Prepare protocols for bibliographic and item standards.
2. Organize staff for an in-house retrospective conversion effort, or,
3. Prepare and distribute requests for vendor-supplied retrospective conversion proposals.
4. Evaluate vendor responses and select a vendor.

Figure 9–1 *Continued*

PHASE 4: SYSTEM SPECIFICATIONS AND REQUIREMENTS

Goal: To prepare and distribute a Request for Proposal (RFP), with specifications, for an integrated, online system.

Tasks:
1. Write specifications for a system based on service priorities.
2. Incorporate specifications into an RFP document.
3. Distribute RFP to appropriate vendors of integrated library systems.

PHASE 5: ANALYZE PROPOSALS AND SELECT VENDOR

Goal: To analyze vendor responses to the RFP and to select a vendor to implement a system.

Tasks:
1. Evaluate vendor proposals.
2. Communicate with vendors for follow-up information.
3. Set up system demonstrations, interviews with vendor clients, or visits to existing vendor sites.
4. Select a vendor.

PHASE 6: CONTRACT NEGOTIATIONS

Goal: To negotiate a favorable purchase contract with the selected vendor.

Tasks:
1. Involve legal counsel, together with library personnel, in the drafting or evaluation of a contract.
2. Bring negotiations to a successful and favorable conclusion.

PHASE 7: SYSTEM IMPLEMENTATION

Goal: To install the selected system.

Tasks:
1. Customize the vendor's system to the library's policies.
2. Physically prepare the library site.
3. Install and test the hardware, software, and telecommunications.
4. Acquire the necessary forms, supplies, and equipment.
5. Load and index the library's bibliographic, item, and patron databases (includes database deduplication in the case of system migration).
6. Train and reeducate staff; realign workflow and space.
7. Activate and evaluate operation of the system.

you will ever need (which will cost you more money.) See Figure 9–2 for a sample statistical profile table.

- The **computer workstation count** is a critical element of your library's profile. System costs hinge directly on the number of computers you plan to deploy for staff, for the public, and for specialized purposes. In establishing projections, here is where you must consider certain issues, if you have not already done so:
  - ➤ You must make an assessment of the **number of computer workstation**s you will need, particularly in public areas. There are no conclusive formulas for determining this. However, taking a survey of the number of workstations in use at certain busy times, the number of people waiting to use occupied machines, or the queue at the card catalog (if your library is not yet automated), will provide useful data.
  - ➤ You must decide how many computers you plan to deploy for specialized purposes, such as:
    - ❏ "ADA-compliant" computers for **disabled users,** that is, those meeting the requirements of the Americans With Disabilities Act, with special adaptive technologies and accessibility features
    - ❏ workstations in **remote locations** (for example, shopping malls) outside of the library (Keep in mind that with browser catalogs, remote workstations that have access to the Internet need not be directly connected to your system)
    - ❏ specially designed **self-service circulation workstations** with scanners and printers for patrons wishing to check out materials themselves
  - ➤ For all the above, remember that you will have to provide appropriate **furniture,** some with special features (such as units for the ADA-compliant machines). Furniture is beyond the scope of this book; it is mentioned here as a reminder that when you make projections and calculate costs, include ancillary expenses such as tables, chairs, and other furnishings for your equipment.
  - ➤ Decide if any of your public workstations will be **thin client machines.** Thin client networks were discussed briefly in Chapter 8. Thin client devices do not have hard and floppy drives or other components found in a personal computer. The applications are stored on the network server.

    Because the thin client consists of little more than a monitor, keyboard, and mouse, it has fewer parts to fail and so may be more reliable than a PC. Transmission speeds may be faster because it sends only small batches of information to the server where the actual processing occurs. Thin clients are easier to set up and do not require frequent installations and upgrades of software clients because these reside on the server. They are also more secure since they are not vulnerable to viruses and other security risks. The disadvantage of thin clients is that because they are not full-fledged personal computers, they lack processing power and the ability to exercise control over applications and data. For example, applications such as MS-Word may not run as efficiently on a thin client; without even a floppy drive it is difficult to save files and other data.

When evaluating the use of thin clients, consider also the mix of applications being made available on public workstations. Choosing to use thin clients means that these workstations will not provide access to all services available. Some libraries may choose to split services even on full-fledged PCs—for example, offering access to the library's catalog and reference databases, but not complete access to the Internet or to word processing, on certain machines. Determining the best method to split services among public machines, however, becomes even more difficult as library catalogs and databases are more inextricably tied to browsers and access to the Internet Web. Thin clients, though, do by their nature improve the library's ability to limit access to a subset of services.

➤ Last but not least regarding computers . . . If you have **computers that you plan to use with your new system,** remember to include these in your count *and* describe your equipment in detail, including make and model, amount of memory and storage capacity, as well as specifications for any internal drives and related peripherals.

• Finally, there are special issues to consider if your library is **migrating** from another vendor's system and **transferring data.** You must describe your databases in detail. Not all vendors have experience transferring data, while some vendors already have developed software to convert records from a previous vendor's system to the new vendor's system. All of this is particularly important if your library's data do not comply with the MARC standard (see Chapter 16) or if you hope to transfer data for which there is currently no standard in place, such as borrower and transaction records.

Figure 9–2   A Sample Statistical Profile of the Library

(Name of Library)_____

	Current	3-Year Projection
a. Estimated number of items in collection		
Print		
Nonprint		
b. Estimated number of titles in collection		
Print		
Nonprint		
c. Number of journal titles		
d. Estimated number of borrowers		
e. Annual circulation		
f. Estimated number of new acquisitions per year		
Print items		
Nonprint items		
Print titles		
Nonprint titles		
g. Staff workstations		
h. Public workstations		
i. ADA-compliant workstations, staff and public		
j. Self-service circulation workstations		
k. Number of workstations in remote locations		

DESIGNING SPECIFICATIONS

In translating your priorities into specifications—articulating what you want your integrated system to do for you—it is important that you think in terms of the *whats*, not the *hows*. Just as you do not have to know how cruise control works in order to know what it does for you as you drive down the highway, you do not have to understand the inner workings of an automated system in order to verbalize what you want out of it.

In essence, specifications define the capabilities that you want in a system. Specify and prioritize attributes ranging from the required (if it's not there, you won't buy the system) to the desirable (nice to have, but you can live without it). Specifications also cover technical areas such as standards that must be adhered to, system operation, maintenance, and system and data security.

Developing clear and accurate specifications that are particular to your library is one of the most important, if not *the* most important, of the activities you will engage in as you plan for your integrated system. These specifications will carry you through the entire procurement process. The system that most closely matches them will be the most useful and the most responsive to your needs.

Development of your system specifications again presents an opportunity to involve key staff who will ultimately be responsible for the successful implementation and operation of your system. This very specific—sometimes tedious—process will build a broader understanding of the technology and its capabilities. It will also force you to identify those functions and features that are essential, as decisions must be made regarding those specifications that are absolutely mandatory. These decisions will be critical at the evaluation stage.

Figure 9–3 provides a checklist of specifications common to most current library systems. To these should be added the specific functions identified through your priority setting. *HINT*: Make each specification as specific as possible. A broader specification covering a number of features may be harder to evaluate if vendors respond that they partially meet such a specification.

Figure 9–3 A Sample Specifications Checklist

GENERAL SPECIFICATIONS

1. The system must be real time and graphical.
2. The system design must be client/server-based employing objects and standard relational database management systems.
3. The system must be written in a common programming language, utilize a recognized processing standard, and run on a standard network operating system or systems.
4. The system must provide seamless, flexible functionality emphasizing streamlined, simple workflows among functional processes.
5. Information, including bibliographic, must be exportable and importable in multiple formats and in both merged and separate files.
6. The system must have the ability to provide a full recovery from any type of system failure through backup or data redundancy.
7. The system must allow for the addition of workstations and the expansion of features without requiring major system redesign or replacement of hardware.
8. The system must function in an internetworking environment through local, wide, or metropolitan area networks, with access to the Internet and the World Wide Web utilizing broadband network services.
9. The system must support remote access through a Web-based interface.

FUNCTIONAL PROCESSES

User Access

1. The system must support a graphical user interface that is common to both on-site and remote users.
2. The system must support multiple search modes geared to the user's proficiency and skill.
3. The system must support multiple locally stored databases, both textual and digitized.
4. The system must support and retain customized personal profiles and preferences for individuals, including screen layout, search histories, and current awareness search strategies.
5. The system must support individual, protected access to user-specific information.
6. The system must provide the capability for individual users to perform unmediated services, such as placement of reserves and interlibrary loan requests, self-checkout of library materials, and interaction with document delivery services, either fee-based or subsidized.
7. The system must support the linkages required to seamlessly search, with one search command, simultaneous, multiple databases located on-site or at remote locations, and in the case of a shared system, to limit searches to specific groups of libraries or outlets.
8. The system must provide online searching aids, such as spell checkers, dictionaries, and thesauri.

Figure 9–3 *Continued*

9. The system must support the use of automated helpers and online aids to assist in search refinement.
10. The system must support natural language searching, relevancy ranking of searches, and the use of controlled authorized vocabulary.
11. The system must support printing, downloading, and exporting of search results to disk files, paper, or into other software applications.
12. The system must support the seamless integration between local and global databases and tools.
13. The system must support the use of the system by the blind or physically challenged.
14. The system must provide customized management reports on user access to the system.

User Services

1. The system must support the circulation of materials, including charge, check-in, renewal, and holds for users through direct borrowing or intra-/inter-library loan.
2. The system must support the creation and circulation management of collections tailored for specific user needs, such as reserve rooms, bookmobiles, rental or rotating circuit collections, collections delivered to shut-ins, and media scheduling and distribution.
3. The system must support the generation of both defined and customized (utilizing a report program generator) reports and notices for both public and staff users. All reports must be available through screen display, in hard copy, and via e-mail.
4. The system must support the registration and management of users, including delinquencies, blocks, fines, receipt generation, and updating of patron information.

Resources Management

1. The system must support the full MARC 21 standard and all previous versions, and all MARC 21 bibliographic records and associated formats, holdings, authorities, and bibliographic and data element standards.
2. The system must support major authorities and thesauri—including Library of Congress Name and Subject Authorities, Medical Subject Headings, and Sears— as well as major classification systems such as DDC, LC, and SuDoc.
3. The system must support import and export of bibliographic records from all major bibliographic utilities, for example, Bibliofile, Marcive, OCLC, RLG, and any other Z39.50-compatible source.
4. The system must support the seamless creation and linkage of item information.
5. The system must support full editing of all the information stored in the catalog records.
6. The system must support the ability to utilize data within the catalog record (for example, a Uniform Resource Locator (URL)) to hyperlink to and access hard-copy, electronic, and multimedia materials, both locally and remotely stored.

Figure 9–3 *Continued*

7. The system must support Dublin Core and Open URL for the purpose of cataloging and maintaining Web sites, both internal and external, as bibliographic metadata.

8. The system must support the electronic procurement of materials, the verification of order data, linkages between order records and fund accounts, and multiple order types, including blanket and standing orders, and deposit accounts.

9. The system must be able to display "on order" information in response to a search query.

10. The system must support the receipt, invoicing, and check-in of materials, including periodicals, standing orders, and bindery returns.

11. The system must track and generate claims for materials or issues not received.

12. The system must generate reports, both predefined and customized, that cover all statistical and management aspects of the control of materials, their purchase, receipt, processing, and use.

13. The system must support a fund accounting system that tracks and accounts for materials expenditures.

Other Resource Management Capabilities

1. The system must provide for the local creation of searchable information files.

2. The system must provide for a conference or meeting room booking capability.

STANDARDS

1. The system must accommodate such formats as the Dublin Core Metadata Element Set, HTML, SGML, XML, TIFF, GIF, JPEG, MPEG, Java, and ActiveX.

2. The system must comply with applicable ANSI, ISO, and NISO standards.

3. The system must accommodate the full ASCII, MARC 21/ALA, and non-Roman/CJK (Chinese/Japanese/Korean) character sets.

4. The system must support appropriate communications and electrical standards and protocols.

SECURITY

1. The system must provide security to prevent accidental or unauthorized modification of records.

2. The system must include safeguards that make it impossible for any person using a workstation to destroy an entire file.

3. The system must provide tiered, password-controlled structures of authorization for applications and operations use that are independent of each other.

4. The system must produce hard-copy notices of items held by borrowers; notices must be printed so that no borrower information is visible.

PREPARING THE REQUEST FOR PROPOSAL

Once you have determined what you want an automated system to do for you and have translated your needs into specifications, you are ready to begin the actual process of procuring a system. If you are in a public institution, you are subject to a bevy of public laws that require purchases of this type to be offered publicly in a competitive manner. This may mean that you will have to go through a formal procurement process in order to acquire your system. This highly structured process usually begins with the issuance of a *Request for Proposal (RFP)* that incorporates your specifications into a document that can be used to objectively evaluate the best proposal for your library system.

In most cases, public institutions are able to issue *Requests for Proposal* instead of *Requests for Bid* (RFB). An RFB implies a very restrictive procurement requiring the library to negotiate with the bidder who meets the minimum requirements at the lowest cost. Procurements based on RFPs are generally preferable to those based on RFBs because you can consider noncost factors such as the overall suitability of the system. Your local purchasing regulations will stipulate how you must proceed.

If yours is not a public institution, you may feel that you can skip this entire process. While you are not legally bound to issue an RFP, it is still in your best interest to undertake the process. Releasing an RFP and requiring vendors to respond to it in a standardized fashion allows you to compare products in a systematic and methodical manner.

It is very difficult to compare systems sensibly and pragmatically solely by viewing vendor demonstrations, talking to sales representatives, reading literature, or comparing broad cost quotations. Using an RFP to solicit written responses allows you to compare functionality, cost, maintenance, support, and all the other issues that are involved in system procurements. The process can save you money and will, in all likelihood, result in a wiser decision.

Your specifications form the basis of your RFP. If you are preparing an RFB, the language, much of it "boilerplate," will be dictated by your local purchasing authorities. You will, however, be able to insert your specifications in the appropriate spots in the document.

The rest of this chapter presents an outline of an RFP for an online, integrated, automated system. As with the specifications, your RFP should be tailored to your own situation; for example, if you are purchasing software only, then you will have shorter sections on hardware.

Figures 9–4 through 9–7 show additional sample forms you might append to the RFP. These include:

- *Notice of Intent to Respond Form*, used by a prospective vendor to inform the library that a proposal is forthcoming (Figure 9–4)
- *System Specification Response Form*, a sample page from the RFP listing specifications (in this instance for the cataloging function) —for libraries wishing to include this level of detail—to which the vendor must respond indicating availability (Figure 9–5)
- *Products and Services List Form*, onto which the vendor is asked to list products and services required for the system; the form should request information on hardware, principally servers and associated peripherals (for example, printers), software, and vendor services (for example, database conversion services) (Figure 9–6)
- *Price Quotation Form*, where the vendor is to list prices for the items on the Products and Services List Form (Figure 9–7)

REQUESTING PROPOSALS FOR AN AUTOMATED, INTEGRATED LIBRARY SYSTEM: AN OUTLINE

INTRODUCTION
Background Information on the Library
1. Statement of purpose regarding automation
2. Narrative profile of the library (for example, collection size, circulation, patron count)

General Rules and Conditions for Submission
1. Overview (library's technology goals and objectives)
2. Schedule of activities (timeline for project)
3. Submission of proposals
   a. Number of copies to be submitted and to whom
   b. Due date

    c. Due date for submission of Notice of Intent to Respond Form (see Figure 9–4)

Proposal Format
1. Arrangement
    a. Responses must follow RFP's format and enumeration.
    b. Required forms must be utilized, filled out, and returned.
    c. Specified standard descriptors must be used (see below for examples).
    d. User and systems operation documentation must accompany proposal (specify number of copies).
    e. Marketing and technical literature and other reference materials may accompany proposal, but must be packaged separately from the response.
    f. Vendors must respond to all functional, technical, and performance requirements in the RFP, and responses must be understood without reference to other documents.
2. Standardized descriptors (to be used to respond to functional and technical specifications and other requirements and specifications as appropriate):
- "In general release"—in production at all user sites. If the function is available always at all user sites and some users choose not to use this function, consider the function in general release.
- "In testing"—in testing and evaluation either in-house or at user sites. Indicate the expected date for general release.
- "In design"—in detailed definition, design, programming, and so forth.
- "In planning"—in general requirements definition or early planning
- "Not available"—not expected to be in a future release or will require special programming at the library's expense to provide.

INSTRUCTIONS TO VENDORS
Letter of Introduction
1. Signed by an officer of the firm
2. Name and address of the firm
3. Name, address, and phone number of authorized contact

Vendor's Company
1. Description of company organization and staffing
2. Resumes of key staff

Vendor's Financial Stability
1. Audited financial statement for past five years or as many years as company has been in business (if less than five)
2. Access to Dun and Bradstreet report if available
3. Credit references

Management Summary (brief statement of system features)

Qualifications of Vendors
1. Client list
2. Right to visit sites

Signatures
1. Submission with signatures of appropriate company officers
2. Corrections and erasures initialed by person signing the proposal or authorized representative

Proposal Evaluation
1. Scoring criteria:
    a. Compliance with specifications set forth in RFP
    b. Adequacy of server configuration and operating system
    c. Availability of all desired functional processes
    d. Functionality (workflows between functional processes)
    e. Capability for system expansion and upgrading
    f. Cost
    g. Maintenance and support
    h. Training
    i. Documentation
    j. Vendor's past performance, including system migration experience
    k. Vendor's financial and organizational credibility
    l. Overall suitability of the system
2. All proposals evaluated in the same manner

Inquiries
1. Instructions for vendor inquiries

Reserved Rights and Special Requirements (will generally be supplied by purchasing or legal department)

TRAINING AND DOCUMENTATION
Training
1. Levels and types of training provided

2. Description of training program, including trainers, qualifications, methodologies, and schedules
3. Right to copy training materials and videotape training classes

Documentation
1. Number of copies of user and system manuals included as part of system purchase
2. Types of documentation required
3. Policies regarding revisions and upgrades
4. Extent of online help
5. Right to copy manuals for internal use
6. Access to documentation in electronic format for easy adaptation to local needs

SYSTEM SPECIFICATIONS

Vendor must use preformatted response forms (see example in Figure 9–5) and the standardized descriptors described earlier. Specifications developed by the library.

DATABASE CREATION OR MIGRATION

1. Creation of bibliographic database or migration of existing database
2. Creation of item database or migration of existing database
3. Creation of borrower database or migration of existing database.

MAINTENANCE

General Description of Maintenance Services, including
1. Hours of service
2. Turnaround time
3. Availability of an 800 number, e-mail, and Web page to report problems
4. Diagnostics through the Internet or via dial-in
5. Types of service (on-site, part swap-out, or combination)
6. Cost of service including premium rates, if any, for off-hours service

Provisions for activation and termination of maintenance

Maintenance Costs
1. Server hardware maintenance requirements
2. Software maintenance requirements

DELIVERY AND INSTALLATION SCHEDULING AND SITE PREPARATION

Description of delivery and installation methodologies
Description of system site preparation requirements

WARRANTIES

Warranties should be determined in conjunction with local purchasing and legal departments.

COST PROPOSAL

Vendor must utilize Products and Services List and Price Quotation Forms provided with RFP (see Figures 9–6 and 9–7).
Prices and price protection should be determined in conjunction with local purchasing and legal departments

APPENDICES (see Figure 9–2)

1. Library's current and projected (three years) file statistics (for example, title/item count, number of borrowers)
2. Library's current and projected activity statistics (for example, circulation, new acquisitions, new borrowers)
3. Estimates of the location and number of staff, public, and specialized computer workstations
4. Library operating hours
5. Library street and mailing address, telephone and fax numbers, and e-mail and Web address

Figure 9–4 Notice of Intent to Respond Form

Please fill out and return this form no later than _____

(date and time)

Name of Company Responding
to Proposal: _____

Name of Contact Person: _____

Telephone Number of
Contact Person: _____

Signature of Representative
of Company _____

CONFIDENTIAL

Figure 9–5 System Specification Response Form

CATALOGING AND BIBLIOGRAPHIC MAINTENANCE REQUIREMENTS

Bibliographic Database

Bibliographic records in full MARC 21 format,
including all MARC fields, both fixed and variable,
and all MARC bibliographic and holdings formats,
must be supported.

Note: The vendor must provide, as an
attachment and referencing this specification,
a list of the names of all the bibliographic utilities
from which MARC records are currently being
successfully loaded into the system (hereafter
referred to as "said utilities").

The system must accept and be able to
accommodate the loading of MARC tapes as
formatted by said utilities through tape, disk, or
online electronic transfer.

The system must have an interface for said
utilities for the transfer of bibliographic records.

The aforementioned interfaces must transfer
the entire MARC record, including all of the
fixed fields and leader into the system.

The aforementioned interfaces must trap
duplicate records corresponding to those
already in the system's database and send
the duplicates to a suspend file for manual
review and disposition.

Figure 9–6 Products and Services List Form

SYSTEM SOFTWARE

Item	Quantity	Model/Manufacturer	Functional Description

Figure 9–7 Price Quotation Form

SYSTEM SOFTWARE

Item	Quantity	Unit Cost	Total Cost	Maintenance

TOTAL

SOURCES

Amtmann, Dagmar, and Debbie Cook. "Increasing Access to Information and Computer Technology for People with Disabilities Through Public Libraries." 1999 [Online]. Available: http://wata.org/pubs/articles/library-access.htm [2001, May 28].
"At the Washington Assistive Technology Alliance . . . we strongly believe that accessible computer stations in public libraries and other public places considerably increase access to information for people with disabilities. . . . In this paper, we describe our collaboration with the Washington State Libraries and the Gates Library Foundation to place accessible computer stations in public libraries that serve rural and disadvantaged populations."

Boss, Richard W. 1999. "A Model RFP for an Automated Library System." *Library Technology Reports* 35, no. 6 (November-December): 715–820.
"This issue presents the latest version of the *LTR* model or sample RFP (Request for Proposal) for an online integrated library system." The Introduction to the report describes the planning process, including the role of library staff, the procurement process, the value of planning, cooperative planning for a shared system, and the use of consultants. The model RFP itself covers instructions to proposers, general system requirements, detailed functional requirements, a minimum hardware configuration, vendor support, and system testing and reliability requirements.

Cortez, Edwin M. 1987. *Proposals and Contracts for Library Automation: Guidelines for Preparing RFP's*. Studio City, Calif.: Pacific Information Inc., and Chicago: American Library Association.
This book is out of print, but has valuable material on the procurement process, preparing the RFP, and making the final selection. Examples of specifications are provided, although some of these require updating.

DeJoice, Mary Jo, and Pongracz Sennyey. 2000. "Some Issues in Implementing Library Self-Checkout Systems: A Management Perspective." *Illinois Libraries* 82, no. 1 (Winter): 5–8.
"This article aims to survey how the implementation of self-checkout systems may affect library management in general and circulation departments in particular rather then [sic] describe the technical aspects of self-checkout systems. Particular attention will be paid to the system's impact on the workflow of circulation departments and the financial implications involved in implementing it."

Doering, William. 2000. "Managing the Transition to a New Library Catalog: Tips for Smooth Sailing." *Computers in Libraries* 20, no. 7 (July/August) [Online]. Available: www.infotoday.com/cilmag/jul00/doering.htm [2001, May 29].
This article offers strategies on how to accomplish a successful migration from an existing catalog to a new OPAC system. The author looks at deci-

sion-making dynamics and provides a checklist of "Things to Look for When Testing Data."

"EQUINOX: Library Performance Measurement and Quality Management System." Last updated April 12, 2001 [Online]. Available: http:// equinox.dcu.ie/index.html [2001, May 30].
EQUINOX is a project funded by the European Commission to address the need of libraries to "develop and use methods for measuring performance in the new networked, electronic environment." Certain indicators presented offer measurements of user demand correlated with hours of service and the number of computer workstations available to assess the effectiveness of computer workstation provision.

Fisher, Shelagh. 2000. "On the Quality and Usefulness of the Specification in Determining a Customer's Requirements: A Survey of UK Library System Suppliers." *OCLC Systems & Services* 16, no. 4: 168–174.
"A survey of UK library system suppliers was undertaken in January 2000 as part of the UK LIC (Library and Information Commission)-funded HARMONISE Project to determine their views on the quality and useful-ness of the specification in the procurement process. The suppliers indi-cated a number of problems inherent in specifications produced by libraries, such as lack of clarity, poor structure, variables in technical understanding, and with too great a focus on basic functionality (that) has been tried and tested. A model specification of system requirements for libraries is recom-mended."

Leavitt, Dawna. "Thin Client Workstations at the Maine State Library." De-cember 2000 [Online]. Available: www.state.me.us/newsletter/dec00/ thin_client_workstations_at_the_.htm [2001, May 28].
This site briefly discusses "Thin vs. Fat vs. Dumb Terminals" in the context of the Maine State Library's network of IBM thin client workstations.

Lisiecki, Christine. 1999. "Adaptive Technology Equipment for the Library." *Computers in Libraries* 19, no. 6 (June) [Online]. Available: www. infotoday.com/cilmag/jun99/lisiecki.htm. [2001, May 28]
This issue of CIL is devoted to "computer technology that can enable the disabled." The article cited here describes adaptive technology—hardware and software—that is "useful in a library setting." Sidebars offer informa-tion on adaptive technology Web sites and vendors.

Martin, Ron G. 1992. "OPAC Workstation Evaluation: The Third Time Around at Indiana State University." *Library Hi Tech* 10, no. 3: 45–54.
This article reports on the findings of surveys conducted at the ISU Librar-ies. The purpose of the surveys was to assess how well the OPAC worksta-tion (computer and furniture enclosure) was meeting users' present needs, to provide guidance in the construction of future workstations, and to de-termine how to better arrange equipment that was part of the present con-figuration.

Miles, J. B. "Thin Clients." October 2, 2000 [Online]. Available: www.gcn.com/vol19_no29/guide/3040–1.html [2001, May 28]
Posted on the Government Computer News.com site, this article discusses the pros and cons of thin client computing and offers a "Tips for Buyers" sidebar.

Morris, Anne, and Hilary Dyer. 1998. *Human Aspects of Library Automation.* 2nd ed. Brookfield, Vermont: Gower.
In the context of the health and safety issues involved with the use of computers, this book includes chapters on workstation components (furniture and computer peripheral equipment), workstation layout and design, and on the environmental considerations—heating, ventilation, and noise—that impact on workplace design.

Reader, Evan A. 1989. "Competitive Procurement of Integrated Library Systems." *Library Hi Tech* 7, no. 2 (Issue 26): 7–15.
"The procurements (at California State University) demonstrated that competitive bidding not only is highly effective in reducing the overall cost of library systems, but also allows the buyer to achieve favorable contract provisions that would be difficult if not impossible to obtain in a noncompetitive environment."

"Sample Request for Proposals (RFPs) and Requests for Information (RFIs) for Library Automation Projects." Integrated Library System Reports. March 28, 2001 [Online]. Available: http://ilsr.com/sample.htm [2001, April 7].
This site is an excellent source of links to actual RFPs used by different types of libraries to acquire systems. Also included are links to guides to the RFP process and writing techniques.

Stowe, Melinda.1999. "To RFP or Not to RFP: That Is the Question." Co-published simultaneously in *Journal of Library Administration* 26, no. 3/4: 53–74, and *Information Technology Planning*, edited by Lori A. Goetsch. New York: The Haworth Press.
"Some libraries are moving away from the (RFP), arguing that it is time-consuming, takes too many staff resources, includes more detail than is needed, and results in a final outcome that is no different than if the system were selected in a more streamlined fashion. This article argues that the benefits of the RFP greatly outweigh other approaches. It also explores the University of Rochester's adoption of the RFP methodology and highlights successes with the model as well as aspects that could be strengthened."

10 EVALUATING PROPOSALS AND SELECTING A SYSTEM

HOW DO YOU MAKE THE FIRST CUT?

Once you have received vendor proposals, it is time to begin the process of system evaluation and selection. The first step is to form a project team to assist you—hopefully including people who have some knowledge of technology or who work in the area(s) being impacted by the system implementation.

You will have read some articles, stopped by vendor booths in exhibit halls, and perhaps requested literature and general cost information from vendors whose products look interesting; *but it is the RFP that will be the cornerstone of your evaluation process*. Thus, if possible, try to wait until you have received all or most vendor responses to your RFP and have had the opportunity to give them an initial look-through before taking the next step, which is to schedule system demonstrations. By so doing, you will avoid having to look at a system that is eliminated early in the evaluation process either because the vendor chose not to respond or because the response was "fatally flawed."

Responses can be fatally flawed for a number of reasons:

- Sections or conditions required by a legal department or by purchasing regulations may be missing or unmet.
- Critical sections of the document may not have been responded to—for example, the vendor did not reply to any of the technical specifications.
- For a software-only purchase, the RFP may have specified that the system must run on specific hardware or a specific operating system and the vendor's software cannot.
- The system's software may be missing the applications functionality that is your number-one priority or one of a number of key functionalities that you have defined in your RFP as absolutely essential.

Problems such as these immediately eliminate a system from further consideration. It is critical, however, to be absolutely sure that the flaw is a fatal one before using it to eliminate a vendor from consideration at the outset. Once any fatally flawed responses have been removed, it is time to schedule system demonstrations and begin in-depth reading of the remaining proposals

SYSTEM DEMONSTRATIONS

Demonstrations are an important component of the evaluation process. You must therefore make the demonstrations as objective as possible and make it as easy as possible for those participating to be able to compare the different systems being demonstrated.

Each vendor has a standard canned demonstration that is meant to show off the system in the most attractive light, highlighting its strengths and camouflaging its weaknesses. It is in your best interest, of course, to see demonstrations that expose the warts as well as the jewels. To do so, allow the demonstration to proceed, then bring out your list of what you want to see demonstrated along with scripted questions you would like answered. It is essential to have your list and questions prepared in advance, and to *use the same list and questions with each vendor.* Again, this allows you to compare more easily how the systems work as well as how they look and feel. Additional questions will probably arise during each demonstration, and will vary with each vendor, making them less easy to compare. That's okay, as long as your preset questions are answered as well.

It is important that as many of the same people as is possible attend all of the demonstrations. If too many people in your evaluation group have not seen all of the systems, it will be difficult to compare them effectively. Also remember that a number of negatives unrelated to the system's performance can affect a demonstration. A nonworking phone line or an inexperienced sales representative can result in a disappointing demonstration of what may in reality be a good system for your needs. Demonstrations are an important part of the evaluation process, but they should always be kept in perspective and should not be the overriding reason for selecting or eliminating a system.

ANALYZING VENDOR RESPONSES

By far the most time will be spent analyzing the vendors' written responses. Now is the time to sit down with the RFP and each response.

SITE CALL HINTS

1. Try to speak with the system manager or automation project coordinator. In most cases, this will not be the director.
2. Explain that you have a number of questions, so that the call may take some time. Encourage short, concise answers, but really informative answers may require some detail.
3. Remember that a fair, unbiased survey is guaranteed by asking each site called all of the questions on the list.
4. Keep in mind that there is a lot to find out, and the calls will require an investment of time. Remember, however, that some of these calls are taking the place of formal site visits, which would be even more time consuming.

- Have pencil and paper or your notebook computer handy.
- Carefully read every response and note any deviations from the requirements as defined by the RFP.
- Note any aspect that is handled unusually well.
- Make a list of any parts of the response that are not clear. These will eventually be turned into a list of written questions to which each vendor will be required to respond in writing.

ANALYZING COSTS

The cost portion of the response may be the most difficult to analyze. Depending on the complexity of your system and the number of libraries participating, consider the use of a spreadsheet in order to evaluate the cost breakdowns.

Costs may not be what they seem at first glance. It is not uncommon for the vendor that appears to offer the lowest cost to end up being the most expensive. When comparing costs, it is critical that you compare apples to apples. Requiring vendors to use preformatted forms designed by you makes the task somewhat easier, but it may take a fair amount of digging to discover whether the low-cost vendor is indeed providing the same range of service or material as the more expensive ones.

TEAM EVALUATION

As noted, it is helpful to have more than one person evaluating the responses. You will want to set up a proposal evaluation team if you have not already done so by this time. Request multiple sets of the proposal itself; however, single copies of manuals, documentation, sample contracts, and so forth, are sufficient. Make sure that your purchasing and legal departments have their own copies of all needed materials.

CALLING VENDOR CLIENTS

Before actually beginning to evaluate the proposals, you will want to call some of each vendor's current clients. The easiest way to have this information at your fingertips is to ask each vendor to provide a client list that includes library type, collection size, size of borrower file, server model and configuration, and the particular software application being used. As with the vendor demonstrations, it is important to have a list of questions ready in advance so that the same questions are asked of each site that is called. (See the Site Call Hints sidebar and the sample Vendor Client Question List in Figure 10–1.)

Be selective in deciding which clients to contact. Generally speaking, call sites of the same library type(s), and of similar size, where the server and software that have been proposed to you are *currently* in use.

Figure 10–1 Vendor Client Question List

Date _____

Library _____

Vendor/System _____

Contact _____ E-mail_____

Telephone _____

1. Describe the system's configuration:

   Telecommunications/network structure

   _____

   Server _____Amt./memory _____ Amt./disk storage _____

   Number of installed workstations _____ Functions (cataloging, circulation, OPAC) being used

   _____

2. What is the size (number of records) of your:

   Bib. file _____Item file _____ Borrower file _____

3. What do you like best about the system?

4. What, if anything, would you most like to change in the system?

5. What problems do you have in using the system?

6. How well does the vendor meet time frames for enhancements, new developments, or changes?

7. Does the vendor supply good documentation for the system and for upgrades? Have you had any problems with the vendor's new software releases?

8. Is the system user friendly? How easy or hard is it to learn and to train staff and patrons to use it?

9. Is system response time acceptable? Is there deterioration during peak hours of use, during report compilation, or as a result of adding more workstations?

10. Do your vendors respond quickly and effectively to reported problems?

11. Why did you choose this system?

Figure 10–1 *Continued*

12. How many staff members run your system? What are their functions? Is the number sufficient?

13. How effective is accessing the Internet, other systems, and remote electronic resources through your system? Is Internet access available to the public directly?

14. Is your vendor providing the appropriate technical assistance you need to establish interfaces with other systems?

15. Can your system export both bibliographic *and* item files in MARC format, integrated in a single bibliographic record? Have you satisfactorily exported bibliographic records and associated item information?

16. What problems, if any, did you encounter during conversion? How did the vendor respond to these or any other problems?

17. Have you applied name and subject authority control to your bibliographic file? If yes, what are its strengths and weaknesses? If not, why not?

18. Are your authority records in MARC format? How do you import and export them to and from your system?

19. How many titles and items do you add to your collection per year? What methods do you use to add bibliographic records to your database? Please evaluate their efficiency and effectiveness.

20. Do you use the acquisitions and serials functionality? If yes, what are their strengths and weaknesses?

21. Do your users find the OPAC easy to use? If not, why not? Is it graphical? Browser-based?

22. What special features are available that are specifically designed for use by children? How would you describe their strengths and weaknesses?

23. Do you get reports through the system? Are you satisfied with them? Are canned reports sufficient, or do you need an optional report generator to get satisfactory reports?

. . . BUT THERE ARE NO VENDOR CLIENTS!

What do you do if the vendor has no current installations of the proposed system or has installations that are not in libraries similar to yours? If the vendor's proposal is sufficiently intriguing and appears to address your needs, you should not automatically reject the proposal, particularly if there are installed sites somewhere. However, you may be willing to consider being a beta-test site for a completely new, never previously installed system or for a system that is being beta-tested at other installed sites. This may be particularly appealing in cases where the proposed system is new but where the vendor has a strong reputation associated with an older system. Also, you may be impressed with a system's functionality or by the vendor's cost proposal for being willing to act as a beta-test site. These are sufficient reasons for allowing vendors to "make the first cut."

SITE VISITS

We discussed site visits earlier as a method of identifying system implementation options and exploring possibilities. They may also be part of the formal selection process.

Because of the time and expense involved, site visits are generally reserved for your top two or three choices. In most parts of the country, it will be possible to identify libraries you want to visit that are within a day's drive, making site visits well worth the effort. As with vendor demonstrations and client calls, a script should be developed in advance and used with each visit in order to insure consistency and thoroughness.

MAKING THE FINAL CUT

Proposals have been read and analyzed, references have been called, and demonstrations have been held. Now it is time to make the final decision.

Members of the evaluation team should meet with their marked-up copies of vendor proposals, their notes on demonstrations and telephone calls, and any other information they may have. Plan to spend the day reviewing everything. Prior to beginning the review, you should have gone over the evaluation criteria you outlined for vendors in your RFP and assigned each criterion a point value. (See the sample Vendor Proposal Scoring Sheet in Figure 10–2.) The total number of points may equal more than 100. The highest point value should be given to "overall suitability of

Figure 10–2 Vendor Proposal Scoring Sheet					
CRITERIA	**POINT VALUE**	**VENDORS**			
		#1	#2	#3	#4
Compliance with overall RFP specifications	(05)				
Availability of desired functional processes	(20)				
Functionality (workflow between and among functional processes)	(10)				
Vendor's past performance	(10)				
Vendor's financial/organizational credibility	(05)				
Adequacy of server configuration and operating system	(10)				
Capability for system expansion	(10)				
Cost *	(20)*				
Maintenance and support	(10)				
Training	(05)				
Documentation	(05)				
Overall suitability of the system	(30)				
TOTALS	(140)				

*Alternatively, as discussed in this chapter, the *Cost* criterion may be held aside and considered separately after a preliminary decision is made based upon the other criteria.

the system," since it encompasses all aspects of the system. The other criteria should be weighted based on their relative importance.

The team then assigns a score to each criterion against which each system is being evaluated. All of the information that has been derived from the proposals, the demonstrations, and the customer calls must be considered in making these decisions. Some scores will be assigned quickly; others will require much discussion and debate before a consensus is reached.

When each system has received scores for each criterion, total the individual scores to determine the system's final score. The system with the highest score becomes the number one finalist, the system with the second highest score is number two, and so on. Using this scoring technique brings a strong dose of objectivity into what is a very subjective process, and provides a consensus-building structure for the library's decision-making process.

Because individuals may interpret vendor responses differently and on occasion incorrectly, a two-step process may also be used in assigning numeric scores. In this "delphi" process, individual scores are tallied, followed by discussion, clarification, and an opportunity for individuals to adjust scores up (or down) in a second—and final—tally. Take the time to make sure that your process and paperwork are organized, that tallies add up, and that supporting documentation is retained.

In many places, procurement processes now provide for a two-step selection process, in which functional components, vendor reliability and support, and overall suitability are rated independently of cost considerations, so that cost does not "overshadow" functionality. In this approach, costs are examined only after the proposals have been ranked and a first choice selected. In this alternative approach, costs of proposals are submitted separately in sealed envelopes, and the envelopes opened only after the review is completed.

A word to the wise: To maintain a negotiating edge, it is better to cut to two vendors rather than one. If that is impossible, maintain the illusion of competition anyway. Remember, the selection process is not over until the contract is signed. Until that point, never let any vendors know that they have been eliminated, including those with fatal flaws. Maintain the confidentiality of the procurement at all times by not discussing the status of individual vendors with others outside the selection team. Be responsive to vendor representatives, but not in such a way as to compromise the integrity of the process.

This is not unlike a job search. Candidates are not sent rejection letters until the final candidate has accepted the offer and has been officially hired. The same is true of automation vendors. Until one has been officially chosen and everyone has signed on the dotted line, do not burn your bridges by rejecting the others. If negotiations with your first-choice vendor fall through, you may want to be able to approach your second and third choices.

SOURCES

American Library Association. *Library Systems Newsletter* (monthly—12 issues) and *Library Technology Reports* (bimonthly—6 issues).
These publications provide useful information on integrated systems, although their scope is broader. *LSN* offers "the latest news of vendors and library technology," and includes an annual survey of vendors. Issues of *LTR* provide overviews of current technology or a comparative evaluation of available products. Both are marketed under ALA's *TechSource (www.techsource.ala.org)*.

Barry, Jeff. 2001. "Closing in on Content." *Library Journal* 126, no. 6 (April 1): 46–58.

———. 2000. "Delivering the Personalized Library." *Library Journal* 125, no. 6 (April 1): 49–60.
These are *LJ*'s "Automated System Marketplace" articles for the years 2001 and 2000 respectively. "Marketplace" is an annual feature that offers valuable information comparing vendor/system sales and numbers of sites by type of library. As noted in Chapter 7, the 2001 article also includes a discussion of "content providers entering the systems arena." The year 2000 article discusses the ASP model as "a variation on system outsourcing," providing examples from the different vendors.

Cibbarelli, Pamela R., comp. and ed. 2000. *Directory of Library Automation Software, Systems and Services*. 2000–2001 edition. Medford, N.J.: Information Today, Inc.
"Published biennially since 1983, the *Directory* . . . provides detailed descriptions of currently available microcomputer, minicomputer, and mainframe software packages and services." It covers software for library automation, information management, text retrieval, and citation management; automation consultants; retrospective conversion products and services; and includes books, serials, CD-ROMs, and Internet resources on the topic of library automation.

"A Helping Hand for Choosing a Library Information System." May, 1999 [Online]. Available: www.coe.missouri.edu/~is334/projects/Project_URL/implementation.html [2001, March 26].
This Web page is published on the University of Missouri-Columbia Web site. It offers a checklist of questions about vendors and systems, relationships with vendors, evaluation of systems, technical support and response time, training, and networking.

"Maree Millard's Automated Library Systems Tips and Hints." September 24, 2000 [Online]. Available: www.home.aone.net.au/libauto/Tips.html [2001, March 1].

Written by someone with a background in special libraries, these tips are designed to assist librarians working in smaller organizations make decisions "in the very complex exercise of selecting a new integrated library system." The site includes material on planning, questions to ask about the system, the vendor, system support, data conversion, and training. It also includes questions to ask the vendors' client references.

Porter-Roth, Bud. 1999. "Choosing a Vendor: Successful Strategies for Evaluating a Vendor Response to an RFP." *Inform* 13, no. 1 (January): 28–31.

"This article reviews how (vendor) proposals are evaluated and outlines general evaluation criteria that can be used and adopted for most evaluation specifications." The author lists examples of evaluation criteria, offers proposal scoring scenarios, discusses the issue of price vis-à-vis other criteria, and, in general, argues that a well-written RFP will encourage well-prepared vendor responses.

11 PUTTING YOUR SYSTEM INTO PLACE

Now that you have completed the selection process and decided on a vendor and a system, there are a few steps you must take before you can have your system up and running. The first step is that you and your vendor must negotiate and sign a contract. Once the contract is signed, you must implement your system and make provisions for its ongoing maintenance and support.

HOW DO YOU NEGOTIATE A CONTRACT WITH YOUR SELECTED VENDOR?

The purpose of a contract is simple: to document the expectations and obligations, with accompanying safeguards, of both the library and the vendor. The contract is based on the specifications delineated in the library's Request for Proposal and the vendor's response to that proposal.

Contracts vary, of course. All contracts include standard legal clauses pertaining to such things as definitions used in the contract, term of the contract, warranties and remedies, insurance, and so forth. Contracts for systems will contain a mutually agreed-upon *system implementation plan* with a hardware/software installation schedule, provisions for the library's formal *acceptance* of the system, and the setting of an *operational date*. The contract will include schedules covering, among other things,

- vendor database services
- system maintenance and support services
- software licenses
- summary of system costs
- payment for the system by the library

The complexity of the contract will depend upon what you are purchasing. A software-only purchase, intended for a network already in place, may be nothing more than a license agreement similar to those accompanying all such kinds of applications software (for example, word-processing or database software). Such a contract may deal only tangentially with hardware. The purchase of a fully integrated system involving multiple applications, hardware, and telecommunications, however, will result in the most comprehensive of contracts.

WHAT DOES THE CONTRACT DO?

Seldom are the vendor's responses 100 percent in accordance with the library's specifications. Thus, the contract needs to:

- interpret and clarify the differences between a vendor's response and the library's specifications
- formalize pricing and payment schedules
- deal with nonperformance issues and remedies, as well as warranties, vendor bankruptcy, software infringement, and maintenance
- safeguard conformance to any legal requirements necessitated by the library's parent organization or governing board

It is essential that the contract be thoroughly examined by the library's (or its governing body's) legal counsel. Implied and expressed warranties, liquidated damages, limitations to remedies, and rights to reject and revoke are legal issues that are best handled by someone with legal expertise.

It is the library's responsibility, however, to ensure that library-specific issues are addressed and codified within the contract. The best method to ensure this is to draft a tightly written Request for Proposal and then to make sure that it is included in the contract along with the vendor's response. If the vendor has agreed to provide functionality that is not currently available, this should be clearly spelled out in the contract itself.

Here are a few pointers:

- Make sure that your contract ties up loose ends and avoids ambiguity.
- Your contract should define responsibility and liability for as many important problems or contingencies as you can envision.
- Since no contract can cover every minor contingency, be prepared to deal with minor issues as they come up during implementation.
- Your contract should cover all major risks and the major objectives of your system, as you have defined them. In negotiations, make sure any issue that is important to you

is discussed, considered fully, and resolved.
- The contract should define responsibilities and protect your rights. Don't use it as a club to extract concessions from your vendor. Remember that the contract is an important element in what should become a productive working relationship.

PAYING FOR THE SYSTEM

Perhaps one of the most important issues is how the library will pay for the system. Rather than pay for each item as it is received and installed, it is usually easier to set up several benchmarks during the installation. When these benchmarks are reached, the vendor will then invoice the library for a predetermined percentage of the total system cost.

For example, assume there are five benchmarks. When each benchmark is reached, the vendor would invoice the library for 20 percent of the total cost. The library would not pay the final 20 percent until it formally signs off on the "final acceptance" of the system.

The problem is that vendors are often anxious to "front-load" payments, that is, receive higher percentages early on, whereas libraries want to pay as little as possible until the very end, when the system is installed and up and running and the library "accepts" the system. Part of the contract negotiations, then, includes the library and the vendor coming to terms on a mutually acceptable series of percentages.

Keep in mind that although most contract negotiations end successfully, not all proceed smoothly. Talks may break down, positions become intractable. It may be necessary to break off negotiations with the first-ranked vendor and move to the second. Remember: As we stressed previously, the process is never over until it's over, so don't tell any vendors that they have not been selected until contract negotiations have been completed successfully.

Contracts: Some Quick Definitions

These definitions offer a sense of the meaning of certain contract-related legal concepts. Readers are urged to consult legal counsel, standard legal references, or titles cited below for fuller explanations.

Express warranty—any direct affirmation of fact relating to the goods sold, as contained in product descriptions or specifications, demonstrations, contractual provisions, and so forth.

Implied warranty—that of "merchantability," requiring that goods be of average quality for goods of that type. Also, "fitness for a particular purpose," suggesting that the vendor must provide a product that meets the buyer's particular requirements.

Limited warranty—any warranty that is not a "full warranty" is a "limited warranty."

Liquidated damages—amounts stipulated by the parties to a contract as damages for the breach of that contract. Such damages, to be enforceable, must represent a reasonable effort to estimate *actual* damages.

Merger clause—where the written contract is considered the exclusive agreement between the parties and there is a disclaimer of any prior warranties or representations.

Right to reject—buyer's right to reject equipment not functioning properly within a reasonable time and recover both monies paid and certain damages. Right is modified by seller's right to correct problems in a timely manner.

Right to revoke—buyer's right to revoke initial acceptance of goods because of a latent flaw not discovered until later or because promised remedies to deficiencies are unsuccessful.

IMPLEMENTING YOUR SYSTEM

Your contract with a system vendor will include a detailed plan and schedule for implementing the system you have purchased. The vendor may assign a consultant or project manager to help guide your library during the implementation phase. Depending upon the provisions of your contract, the vendor will also assign trainers to instruct your staff on the new system. (Chapter 12 will discuss training issues in more detail.)

In advance of the actual implementation, the vendor's consultant or project manager will likely meet with you to plan the overall project. Special attention will be paid to two critical issues:

- **creating the policy files** (also known as profiling)—essentially, defining your patron types, collection categories, loan periods, and so on, and the matrix that links them all together as the foundation of your system, and,
- **migrating your data**—principally, the library's bibliographic database, but also possibly patron and transaction files from your previous system.

The implementation plan in your contract will delineate and describe

- the key events that must occur
- who is responsible for them (you, the vendor, or both, depending upon your arrangements with the vendor)
- the date the events will occur, usually defined as "X" days from contract signing

Key events will involve, among other steps, the following—depending upon the nature of your procurement:

- site preparation
- data extraction from previous system
- ordering of hardware and software
- implementation and profiling visit by vendor consultant
- hardware installation
- installation of vendor application software
- loading and indexing of databases
- installation of client software
- system training
- acceptance testing by the library, that is, does everything work as it should?
- library goes live on the system
- library acceptance of the system, that is, everything, or most everything, works as it should
- system declared operational

RUNNING AND MAINTAINING YOUR SYSTEM

This is a good place to recall the point made earlier about how the phases of automation planning do not occur sequentially. In fact, key decisions about maintaining and supporting your system will have been made before now, based in part on the outcomes of your initial planning efforts and in part on the options available through your selected vendor.

It should be clear to everyone that implementing a system means more than clearing space on a table for the CPU. Your system is part of an infrastructure, both technical and human, that must be in place in order for your system to perform effectively over time.

FIRST QUESTION: WHO'S GOING TO RUN THE SYSTEM?

At the present time, integrated systems are, for the most part, still managed within the library or parent body, by library or other institutional staff. An alternative approach—your vendor as "application service provider"—was discussed in a previous chapter. We have evolved from the time when all we had to worry about was placing a student assistant, clerical aide, or page with some technical smarts in charge of the CD-changer. However, we are also well beyond the point where an integrated system can be run part-time by the director or a reference librarian. It is now common for certain integrated system vendors to stipulate that the library must designate a full-time system manager and validate the availability of technically certified staff with responsibility for system operations.

Thus, your first basic consideration is to decide who in your organization will be responsible for maintaining the network on which your new library system application runs. This may involve reassigning job responsibilities as well as committing funds for training—over and above the money you are paying your vendor to train your staff on the new system. It means providing training to ensure that your staff is able, among other things, to

- administer a network that has a Unix-based or Microsoft Windows operating system
- install, maintain, and troubleshoot the library's servers and client workstations
- work with the relational database, for example, Oracle,

Figure 11–1 Example of Windows Maintenance Schedule

Area to Maintain	Definition	Task Schedule
Operating System Event Log	Records *system* errors (e.g., hardware problems, driver errors) and *application* errors (e.g., database failures)	Review daily, checking for both types of errors
Registry Backups	Registry stores hardware, software, and user account information	Back up daily and use backup to restore registry if damaged
Emergency Repair Disk	Use to boot system from floppy if system crashes	Update when hardware and software configurations are changed
Available Disk Space	Keep 25 percent free space on server for temporary files	Review weekly; clean up files as needed
Services	Array of operating system services that must run 24x7	Review daily; make sure everything is running
System Log Files	Log of system file activity	Review daily; check for errors; delete old logs
CPU and Memory Usage	Monitor performance—check for sustained spikes in usage and insufficient memory	Review quarterly to determine need for upgraded CPU, more memory

SQL, that runs underneath your system vendor's application

- perform regular system maintenance and backups
- reorganize and rebalance system files and indexes
- maintain logs of system operations
- compile and generate system reports and notices
- develop, implement, and maintain hardware and software inventory and security controls
- maintain firewalls and proxy servers (to authenticate remote users)

- bring the system to a speedy and effective recovery in the event of a system failure

SECOND QUESTION: HOW ARE YOU GOING TO KEEP YOUR SYSTEM RUNNING SMOOTHLY?

The next consideration is: What arrangements are in place with your system vendor and with third-party contractors to maintain your network? A major responsibility of your staff will be to communicate and work with your system software and hardware vendors and your ISP (Internet service provider) to determine what types of maintenance and support are handled by your staff and what kinds of maintenance and support require intervention from your vendor.

It is important to remember that your library application runs on a network that is *yours*, not your system vendor's. That means you bear a major responsibility for the network running smoothly. Thus, if your integrated system runs on Windows, maintaining the Windows operating system is the library's responsibility. Figure 11.1 illustrates a part of what library staff must do to maintain a Windows operating system. This will vary with the version of Windows that you have.

With respect to your vendor(s), questions to consider include:

- **What levels of service are appropriate?**
  Most hardware and software maintenance contracts will give you service 24 hours a day, 7 days a week, 365 days a year with two-hour turnaround time—if you are willing to pay for it. Unless you are running an airline reservation system or the Pentagon, however, such comprehensive service will be way over your budget and probably not really necessary.

  So . . . *know your site.* If you are a busy public library, it may be worthwhile to pay extra for Saturday service or for service after 5 p.m. Also, know your time zone. If your software vendor is in California and you are in New York, the basic service hours may be 7 a.m. to 6 p.m., Pacific Time. For you, this means 10 a.m. to 9 p.m.

- **How is the support service accessed?**
  It is helpful if hardware and software maintenance calls can be placed via 800 numbers and if calls can be made at any time of the day or night. However, there is a growing trend to reporting problems via **e-mail**. Frankly, many service personnel today will more readily check their e-mail

than their voicemail. Discuss this issue with your vendor when you begin your service relationship.

All software maintenance will be accomplished via a dial-up telephone line or through the Internet from your vendor's place of business. This is standard operating procedure and works just fine. However, it is important that the vendor have clearance to access your system through firewalls and other security controls.

- **Can we get on-site service?**
  In the past, it was helpful if your hardware vendor had an office located close to you, a number of field engineers, and an in-depth parts inventory available locally. Today, hardware vendors such as Dell and Gateway often contract with third parties for on-site service.

  It is important to understand that a great deal of your maintenance service will not occur on-site. Service to your central site server hardware and related peripherals may be on-site. However, for the rest of your equipment, such as client workstations, keyboards, printers, telecommunications equipment, and bar-code wands, the vendor will likely send you a replacement while you return the defective unit. This approach has replaced "depot service," whereby if something didn't work, you packed it up, mailed it to a service depot, and waited for it to return in working condition.

- **Should we self-insure?**
  The question of self-insurance always pops up, particularly from parent organizations looking to save money. On the one hand, service contracts are a necessity for your server hardware and telecommunications equipment: This equipment is too expensive to simply replace every time something breaks, and it may not be that easy to find someone to fix the problem if you don't have a contract.

  On the other hand, workstations, and especially keyboards and bar-code scanners, are significantly less expensive. For equipment that is no longer under warranty, it may be worthwhile to set up a fund to finance the purchase of new equipment that is put into service when something breaks down. The alternative is to pay the time-and-materials charges to have repairs made as needed, rather than buy a service contract in advance. If you decide to go this route, be sure that you determine before the fact who will do the "as-needed" repair work and that they will do it on a time-and-materials basis.

- **How do we keep the network secure?**
  Libraries have always dealt with the issue of physical safety and security. With automated systems, networks, and the Internet, a whole new set of issues has arisen for libraries. Just as keeping all your books under lock and key restricts access, so does building electronic "gates" within and around your system inhibit the ability of people to get to all your important resources. However, you must protect the network you have assembled, and its databases, from those who would damage or destroy them. Hence, it is important that you discuss security issues with your vendor.

  Security involves a number of different approaches. **Firewalls** and **proxy servers** are electronic barriers you establish between your network and the outside world, either to keep people out of your network or to authenticate their use of certain functions (for example, access to commercial databases) within it. You can use **passwords** and **TCP/IP** addresses to restrict access to system functions or services and various **software applications**, such as *WinSelect, Everybody's Menu Builder, Fortres*, and *Deep Freeze*, to restrict or prevent the user from freely manipulating the computer workstation's desktop. Finally, **antivirus** programs such as *Norton AntiVirus* and *McAfee ActiveShield* are designed to intercept and eliminate software viruses that can infiltrate files and wreak havoc on hard drives.

  These methodologies and individual products may or may not be compatible with your integrated system or with your network operating system. It is important that you pursue the question of security and the issue of compatibility with your vendor as part of the overall planning for your network's smooth operation and ongoing maintenance.

CONCLUSIONS

It is important to be clear about your system vendor's role in the maintenance process in order to avoid finger-pointing. For example, imagine that your system is down. Upon calling the system vendor and describing your situation, you are told that the problem is with your Internet service provider (translation: call someone else). But the ISP says that the problem is with the system software, so around it goes. Your contract must contain language that specifically defines the system vendor's responsibility for maintaining operations once the system is installed.

Keep in mind, however, that—given the fact that workstations usually serve multiple purposes—your system may be down for reasons unrelated to the integrated system per se. For example, the local area network itself could be down, and the LAN is not the responsibility of the system vendor.

In general, though, effective maintenance arrangements will guarantee that you get the best use out of your system with a minimum amount of downtime. Maintenance specifications should be an integral part of your RFP, and all maintenance arrangements, specifications, and prices should be clearly delineated in your contract. When you need it, you really need it, and you don't want the provisions to be vague or unclear.

SOURCES

Bielefield, Arlene, and Lawrence Cheeseman. 2001. *Library Contracts and the Law*. New York: Neal-Schuman.
"This volume will help librarians understand, negotiate, and avoid the pitfalls of all kinds of contracts that might be used in libraries." Among many other types of contracts and agreements, the book covers maintenance and repair agreements, purchasing contracts, and computer equipment purchase and leasing.

Canavan, John E. 2001. *Fundamentals of Network Security*. Norwood, Mass.: Artech House Publishers.
Although not specifically geared to libraries, this "easy-to-understand book" introduces fundamental network security concepts, principles, and terms. "From LAN/WAN security . . . encryption on the Web . . . to secure e-mail protocols . . . and firewalls, it covers essential topics on network security that can be understood even if you don't have a technical background."

Cortez, Edwin M. 1987. *Proposals and Contracts for Library Automation: Guidelines for Preparing RFP's*. Studio City, Calif.: Pacific Information Inc., and Chicago: American Library Association.
This book, cited previously in connection with RFP preparation and system evaluation, contains useful chapters on "Writing and Negtiating the Contract" and "Examples of Contract Specifications." Some of its references to library automation functionality are dated.

Lavagnino, Merri Beth, comp. and ed. 1997. "System Security in the Networked Library." *Library Hi Tech* 15, no 1–2 (Issue 57–58): 7–102.

"This collection of articles is organized into three sections: Workstation Security, Authentication and Authorization, and Security Breaches. In each section, the authors lay out general issues and techniques and describe real-life development projects, production implementations, and actual experiences." Marshall Breeding's article, "Designing Secure Library Networks," offers several useful designs. Jim Rosachi's "Give Yourself a Break: Don't Give the Hackers One" offers a "Poor Security Checklist Test" to determine your level of security preparation.

Mayo, Diane, and Sandra Nelson. 1999. *Wired for the Future: Developing Your Library Technology Plan.* Chicago: American Library Association.
The Tech Notes section includes material on "Computer and Network Security," pages 150–158.

Pattison, Steven. "Computer and Network Security in Libraries." 1997 [Online]. Available: www.slis.ualberta.ca/s98/steven/sp_secur.htm [2001, February 19].
This paper presents an overview of the ways automated library systems are vulnerable to attack, discusses measures and remedies for ensuring security, and outlines the risks associated specifically with providing access to the Internet.

12 TRAINING! TRAINING! TRAINING!

When thinking of technology planning, there is often a tendency to focus on the hardware and software aspects of planning and to ignore the human aspects of automation—specifically, staff and user training. Without these, the most carefully designed system may not be accepted by library staff or library users. To ensure the success of your hard planning work, a training plan should be part of any technology project.

HOW DO YOU TRAIN—AND RETRAIN—STAFF?

It is important to remember that when we automate, we are not just learning how to use an integrated system; we are in most instances also learning new jobs. This is true even if your library is currently automated and migrating to a different system. Fortunately, educating the staff and orienting them to technology can begin long before the selected system is installed. By involving staff at all levels in the analysis of operations, the identification

---

SECRETS OF SUCCESSFUL TRAINING

To ensure that your training efforts are as effective as possible, the following training tips should be kept in mind:

1. Designate an individual or group of individuals who will work closely with vendor representatives and will have responsibility for ongoing training.
2. Focus on those skills most relevant to day-to-day operations.
3. Work with small groups and provide hands-on experience.
4. Do practice training on a small test group first.
5. Make sure that trainees can go back and actually use the system immediately after receiving training.
6. Always check your equipment, software, and database prior to beginning training.
7. Ask trainees to evaluate training sessions and make changes accordingly.
8. Offer refresher training on a regular basis.

---

of needs, the setting of priorities, the development of specifications, and the evaluation of systems, staff will gain much of the general knowledge they need as the planning progresses.

When developing the RFP, pay particular attention to the section on training:

- Identify and plan your training needs.
- Describe in detail what you expect to receive from the vendor's training program.
- State objectives clearly and ask for a detailed outline of the training offered, including the curriculum, the amount of time spent on each segment, the number of people to be trained at once, and the cost.
- Ask what training aids the vendor provides, such as training databases, manuals, workbooks, indexed and well-organized documentation, computer-aided instruction, instructional videos, and Web-based tutorials. Ask if these can be downloaded or copied for future internal use.
- Request cost information on telephone support and follow-up, on-site training.
- Inquire about videotaping training classes for review and for training of new staff.
- Require output measures that ensure satisfactory proficiency levels.

Evaluate and analyze vendor responses to training questions as critically as you would the responses to hardware and software specifications. Finalize all aspects of the training program as part of the contract negotiations. This is particularly important in system migrations, when staff are being retrained. Determine when and where training sessions will be held, how many will attend each class, what the level and content of each session will be, and what documentation and training aids—including test databases and audiovisual aids—will be provided.

Remember that resistance to change, unlearning old skills acquired from previous manual or automated systems, and longer learning curves are characteristic of many staff trainees. Do not schedule training sessions too far in advance of when the trainees will actually begin to use the system or subsystem. Make objectives and expectations clear in the beginning, and create a nonthreatening training environment.

For initial training, scenarios are particularly useful — "A patron is trying to check out a book but has forgotten her library card" — and staff can enjoy developing them in order to explore system functionality. Encourage creativity on the part of trainers, and remember that staff will learn better—and longer—if they're having fun!

Particularly when retraining staff, ensure that training sessions are geared to the participants' levels of expertise. For staff already skilled in using an automated system, an emphasis on training in the basic aspects of the system may be unnecessary. However, this may not be true when migrating from a text-based legacy system to one with graphical capabilities in which dexterity using a mouse assumes greater importance. Staff used to the keyboard/scanner configuration of a text-based system may feel that adding the mouse into the configuration slows them down and causes them to work less efficiently, particularly in circulation-based functions such as check-out and check-in and fine collection. In fact, the mouse/keyboard/scanner configuration may actually be slower and more cumbersome in these circumstances. Often there are keyboard combinations that can take the place of the mouse, and part of the training class should focus on these faster mouse-alternative sequences.

Provide an introductory overview of the entire system. Encourage procedural and methodological comparisons with the previous system.

In most instances, systems are sufficiently complex that it will be necessary to have certain staff members receive training in specific components of the system. For each such component, identify a staff member who will work closely with vendor trainers initially and will in turn provide ongoing training for other staff members as required. This person should not be the system administrator. In choosing an in-house training coordinator, enthusiasm and interest should be the primary consideration, rather than just computer expertise.

The training coordinator should:

- assess the knowledge and experience of the vendor trainer(s)
- assess in advance the quality and timeliness of the training aids and documentation, rewriting where necessary
- select an appropriate training area
- select staff to be trained and grouped in classes based on criteria such as level of expertise and curriculum to be covered
- identify trainees with an aptitude to become in-house trainers
- communicate with vendor trainer(s) to discuss the level of training needed for each group and the amount of support that will be provided to subsequent in-house training, including follow-up training

SPECIALIZED STAFF TRAINING

The impact of the Internet and the World Wide Web on automated library systems has resulted in the need to train staff in the development and use of tools needed for the creation of a "virtual" library. The creation and design of Web pages requires significant training in the use of electronic authoring tools and data encoding schemes such as HTML and SGML (respectively, HyperText Markup Language and Standard Generalized Markup Language—see Chapter 17). Catalogers must learn to create the MARC field for Electronic Location and Access and link the contents of its subfields, particularly the URL (Uniform Resource Locator), into a Web-browser environment for instant user access to the location specified. Training in these specialized areas may be done in-house but may also require an investment in vendor-run training classes, either on- or off-site.

In all cases, though, it is important to determine what skills your staff currently have and what skills they need to attain to effectively work with the new system. Once these have been established, the challenge will be to combine vendor training programs with in-house efforts to design and implement a strategy that will meet the needs of your staff.

TRAINING AND RETRAINING THE PUBLIC

Public relations is not the first vehicle that comes to mind when we think of training the public, but public acceptance and enthusiasm for your new automated system is an important ingredient in a successful planning effort. Remember that the public, more than ever before, is much more likely to be using technology to provide access to entertainment and information from home, work, and school. Your users will want to know how your system fits into and interacts with the electronic resources and activities that they are already familiar with.

Public relations can accomplish three things:

- It can make users aware of your new system and services.
- It can motivate them to use the system.
- It can train them in using the new system and services effectively.

In developing a training plan, all three of these should be consciously addressed, and each may suggest a different approach.

Public training methodologies will vary with the type of library. They may include:

- developing handouts, flyers, and tip sheets geared to the library's clientele
- formal class instruction, particularly in school and academic libraries
- short, focused minicourses on topics such as system overview, searching strategies, understanding a Web browser, and developing, using, and removing individual user preferences
- use of volunteers, as well as staff, to provide individualized one-on-one help.

Remember, not all training has to occur in the library. Outreach efforts that take place where users live and work can be just as effective—if not more so—than efforts undertaken on-site. These might include workshops in establishing remote connections to your system from home computers and Web-based tutorials, which can be used from home, school, or work on particular aspects of the system that individual users or groups of users will be interested in.

Whenever possible, try to identify specific user groups for whom customized training can be provided, particularly if training can be tailored to the known needs of the group. Such groups might include faculty, friends, community organizations, or groups within your parent organization.

You may also want to explore online tutorials, designed to introduce patrons to basic system features and advanced research techniques. These may be available through the vendor, or may be developed by another library that is using the same system software.

Most vendors pride themselves on their system's intuitive, easy-to-use, public interfaces. Nevertheless, training is important, particularly when it is focused on blending the features of your system with other tools on the Web to create a flexible, full-featured information resource package accessible both inside and outside the library.

CONCLUSION

The following are good guidelines for both staff and public training:

- Involve staff members at all levels in planning activities.
- Evaluate and make effective use of vendor-provided training materials and make sure you receive enough to meet your needs.
- Identify any separate training programs, who will be trained, and individuals who will be responsible for any ongoing training in the area.
- Use training tips to make in-house training effective.
- Integrate Web-based training modules, accessible remotely, into your training modules.

SOURCES

Brandt, D. Scott. 1998. "Compartmentalizing Computer Training." *Computers in Libraries* 18, no. 1 (January): 41–44.
The thesis of this article is that teaching a variety of computer concepts from how to use a mouse to how to construct a Boolean search can be daunting. One approach is to compartmentalize the material into three groups, technology, information technology, and information literacy. Although there will be overlap among the areas, multilevel training can significantly strengthen the teaching and learning of these subjects.

———. 1996. "Training for Automated Systems in Libraries." *Information Technology and Libraries* 15, no. 3 (September): 157–167.
"In a series of interviews, the automation administrators of forty-nine libraries that had recently installed automated systems discussed staff and user training for their new systems. The interviews focused on training objectives and procedures, timing and effectiveness of the training, and problems encountered. Eight vendors then presented their points of view as they responded to issues raised by librarians."

Fidishun, Dolores. "People Servers vs. Information Providers: The Impact of Service Orientation on Technology Training." *Information Technology and Libraries* 20, no. 1 (2001) [Online]. Available: www.lita.org/ital/2001_fidishun.html [May 28].
"This article posits the existence of two categories of service orientation: People Servers (who believe that they must always be present to assist people,

even to the detriment of learning technology), and the Information Providers (who view the learning of new technology a way to assist patrons). Training implications for both types of staff members are discussed and suggestions are made for maximizing the transfer of training for each type of trainee."

King-Blandford, Marcia. 1998. "Training Users for Desktop Access." *Computers in Libraries* 18, no. 1 (January): 51–54.
While this article deals specifically with training students in the College of Engineering at the University of Toledo, Ohio, it offers insights into the development of an instructional Web site for use in training.

Krissoff, Alan, and Lee Konrad. 1998. "Computer Training for Staff and Patrons: A Comprehensive Academic Model." *Computers in Libraries* 18, no. 1 (January): 28–32.
This article presents a model for developing core computer competencies for both staff and patrons. It includes an example of an instructional outline and discusses content and program development.

McDermott, Irene E. 1998. "Solitaire Confinement." *Computers in Libraries* 18, no. 1 (January): 22–27.
The author uses the problem posed by students playing solitaire during instructional sessions as a means of exploring the importance of the physical factor in computer training. Tips and techniques for effective design or redesign of the training environment are featured.

Marmion, Don. 1998. "Facing the Challenge: Technology Training in Libraries." *Information Technology and Libraries* 17, no. 4 (December): 216–218.
Marmion outlines the computer skills now required to function effectively in today's libraries and emphasizes the importance of ongoing training.

Morris, Anne, and Hilary Dyer. 1998. *Human Aspects of Library Automation*. 2nd ed. Brookfield, Vermont: Gower.
This book covers all aspects of human interactions with computers including ergonomic issues and workplace design. Training is discussed in Part VIII. Special emphasis is placed on the importance of ongoing and refresher training, documentation, and descriptions of training methods and content.

Oakland (Calif.) Public Library. "Technology Competencies for Library Staff." Fall 1998 [Online]. Available: www.oaklandlibrary.org/techcomp. htm [2001, May 28].
This document provides "a list of minimum expected technology competencies for nearly all classifications and work locations at the library," including technology skills that *all* staff should have.

Sada, Ellis. 1999. "Training Users in the Electronic Era." *Special Libraries* 3, no. 12 (December): 22–28.

The author, library director at Catholic University, Milan, Italy, discusses training experiences and training techniques used to educate users to more effectively utilize the library's electronic resources and tools.

Tennant, Roy. 1995. "The Virtual Library Foundation: Staff Training and Support." *Information Technology and Libraries* 14, no. 1 (March): 46–49. "The creation, management, and support of virtual libraries require at all stages skillful and knowledgeable support of library staff." This article focuses on instruction and training methods, varieties of documentation used to support training, and staying up to date after training, including remaining aware of what may be possible in the future.

PART III:

PLANNING YOUR IN-HOUSE COLLECTION DATABASES

As noted in Chapter 7, today's integrated systems provide access to materials and databases that are located worldwide, dramatically changing how we think of what constitutes a "local" database or collection. Nonetheless, for most libraries, the collections that physically reside there are often still of primary importance.

That's what the chapters in Part III are about—creating and maintaining your in-house databases. This is important because high-quality, machine-readable databases are the cornerstone upon which so much of your future automation efforts will rest. Vendors may come and go, hardware may become obsolete, software may be replaced, but well-constructed, well-maintained databases will be the library's transportable and viable links from system to system.

The following chapters deal with retrospectively converting manual files to machine-readable ones, maintaining the bibliographic database once it is automated, bar coding your collections, and applying the MARC standard. Standards are a critical part of creating and sustaining high-quality databases. Adherence to standards, including those for collections and for your integrated system itself, is covered in detail in Chapter 17.

13 UNDERTAKING RETROSPECTIVE CONVERSION

WHAT IS RETROSPECTIVE CONVERSION AND WHY IS IT IMPORTANT?

Conversion is the sequence of steps needed to acquire, create, or modify machine-readable records for an automated database. Simply, it is the process whereby records only humans can read are transformed so that computers can read them, too. Converted data may include:

- the card catalog
- the shelflist
- borrower information
- serials check-in records
- citations from indexes
- community information and other referral files
- the text of books and articles
- pictures, illustrations, graphs, and tables
- book and library materials vendor information
- fund accounting information

Most libraries now have very likely retrospectively converted their bibliographic information. However, it is a sad fact that many libraries, particularly those in elementary and high schools and in the corporate sector, may not have created machine-readable files adhering to the full MARC standard. Or, they may have loaded full MARC records into a non-MARC-based system and neglected to continue maintaining their MARC records separately. These libraries, when they make the decision to migrate to a more fully featured and usually MARC-based system, discover to their dismay that they must go through a retrospective conversion yet again. This is because their bibliographic data is not in a standard format and cannot be easily migrated from the old to the new system.

As a result, while a discussion of retrospective conversion may seem like old news, it may in fact be as new as today's headlines—a perfect illustration of the old adage that what goes around, comes around.

This chapter looks at the conversion of bibliographic data files, but it is important to keep in mind other types of data as candidates for conversion. These may include textual citation files used for reference and referral and full-text materials such as reading lists, bibliographies, course syllabi and reserve materials, or catalogs. Image and other graphical files should also be identified and assessed. These types of materials will likely require scanning or direct data entry in order to convert them to machine-readable form. Their accessibility, once converted, will require a graphical rather than a text-based interface, yet another good reason why libraries migrate their data to newer systems with more far-ranging capabilities. (Standards used for conversion of nonbibliographic data are discussed in Chapter 17.)

Conversion of the card catalog and shelflist is a prerequisite to the effective automation of all traditional library functions. The process is similar in some ways to highway repairs: costly, labor intensive, and aggravating to all those involved. But the result—a high-quality, transportable bibliographic database—is worth the temporary inconvenience.

When conversion is undertaken with a library's entire existing collection and current acquisitions, the process is known as *retrospective conversion*. Once you have made the decision to initiate a retrospective conversion project, you must determine the scope of the project by:

- deciding what areas of the collection will be converted
- prioritizing the order in which each area is to be done
- determining the speed with which the conversion must be accomplished

Write down the scope, goals, and objectives of your project, and be sure everyone involved understands them. Staff participation is very important to the success of any retrospective conversion project. Bring your staff into the planning process from the beginning.

PREPARING FOR RETROSPECTIVE CONVERSION

WEEDING AND INVENTORY

Weeding and inventory are crucial precursors to retrospective conversion. Since it costs money to create, process, update, and store each bibliographic record, it is a waste of labor and funds to create records for missing or outdated items.

Weeding can begin now, right this minute. It does not require special funding or budget approvals, but it does require commitment, reallocation of human resources, and adjustments to workflow. On the bright side, weeding will save your library money and time. (A weeding process is described in Chapter 14.)

A physical inventory of the collection is important for two reasons. First, it will prevent conversion of items that have vanished, and second, it is a critical means of comparing the physical item to its "surrogate," in most cases a shelflist card, so that information, both bibliographic and local holdings, can be matched, corrected, deleted, or added. Inventory time is a good time to add unique numeric identifiers such as an LCCN (Library of Congress *Card* Number—not to be confused with the LC *class* number) and an ISBN (International Standard Book Number) or ISSN (International Standard Serial Number) to the shelflist, if they do not already appear. These numbers should be obtained only from the item itself or from a MARC record (MARC—MAchine Readable Cataloging—standards are discussed later). *Books in Print* should not be used as a source for these numbers because the numbers sometimes change. When feasible, both an LCCN and an ISBN should be added to monographs and an LCCN and ISSN to serials. Be wary of using LCCNs printed in paperbacks; they are often for the hardback edition.

Here are examples of the numeric identifiers mentioned above.

LCCN: 65–9908
LC Class Number: Z 1011 .B63 1990
ISBN: 0–8103–0586–0
ISSN: 0524–0581

FILE IDENTIFICATION

It is also important to analyze—to identify, describe, and document—all of the library's manual files that are to be converted. A method for analyzing the shelflist file is presented further on, but don't forget all those other files that lurk in your library, such as:

- serials check-in files
- order files
- borrower files
- overdues
- product files
- clipping files
- resource files for community information or other special purposes.

Without this analysis, it is difficult to determine the costs that will be required not only for a retrospective conversion but also for the automated system itself. You should obtain the following information from this effort:

- how the file is used
- number of records in the file
- types of information contained in each record (for example, for an overdue: title, call number, date due, borrower name, amount of fine; for a serials check-in: title, volume number, issue/part number, date received)
- number of records added, deleted, or changed daily, weekly, monthly, and annually
- methods of file maintenance
- frequency of file use
- extent and type of duplication of information in other files
- how well data elements conform to specific standards (see Chapter 17) and the types of variations that are present

Start looking at your files early on. It is not necessary to examine a file in its entirety. Usually, a sampling is sufficient for collecting the information required for analysis. (For the shelflist, this should be done *after* the completion of a weeding and inventory program, so that missing and discarded titles do not affect the final result.) Analysis of the sample provides the information required to implement the most cost-effective and efficient data conversion method or methods. Different sampling techniques exist for providing a valid sample from which to draw the information that you need (see the *Sources* for further reading), or you may choose to devise one of your own.

UNDERSTANDING METHODS AND COSTS OF CONVERSION

STEPS IN THE CONVERSION PROCESS

It may be useful at this point to briefly outline the actual steps involved in a typical conversion project:

Step 1: Using the information from the library's existing catalog (usually the shelflist but sometimes a non-MARC, machine-readable bibliographic file), the library or a contract service vendor locates matching computerized bibliographic records, generally through a computer search of the MARC database first and other resource databases subsequently.

Step 2: Matching bibliographic records are verified as correct matches, are edited to conform to the cataloging practices of the library doing the converting, are extracted from the resource databases, and are then added to a separate machine-readable collection database for that library.

Step 3: The library (or contractor) then creates machine-readable records for titles in the library's collection *not* located in any of the resource databases. This record is most commonly a full bibliographic record (containing all the information on the 3x5 catalog card or in the machine-readable record), but may be only a short entry.

Step 4: The library's new bibliographic database can now be used as the basis for an automated, integrated system.

DATA CONVERSION METHODS

Data conversion methods most commonly used are:

- in-house conversion, using existing staff
- outsourced in-house conversion, using outside contract labor
- outsourced off-site conversion, with a service vendor doing the keying or machine matching

There are advantages and disadvantages to each of the above methods.

In-house conversions using existing staff

- reduce initial financial outlay, lowering up-front per item costs
- allow files to remain on-site

However, hidden costs such as . . .

- impact on existing workflow
- excessively long timelines for project completion
- additional space and hardware requirements
- added supervisory and quality-control efforts
- increased personnel costs

may in fact make in-house conversions more costly in the long run.

Outsourced in-house conversions using outside contract labor

- allow files to remain in the library
- lessen the negative impact on workflow and staff time

However:

- Space must be found for the additional temporary personnel.
- They must be able to work smoothly with existing staff.
- There must be access to a database against which to match and convert your records (as with any in-house conversion).

This database may be a Web-based online bibliographic utility, a MARC file on compact disk, or software utilizing the Z39.50 information retrieval standard. The Z39.50 standard allows a library to "grab" MARC records from a source such as the Library of Congress and import them into a stand-alone MARC editor or a local system.

Outsourced, off-site vendor-keyed or machine-match conversion

In this method, each item in the collection—as described in the shelflist—is matched to a database owned by the vendor. Alternatively a bibliographic database provided by the library, usually as an extraction from a non-MARC-based local system, may be processed by the vendor, and then run against a MARC bibliographic file.

NOTE

As stated earlier, most libraries convert their collections from their *shelflists*. Shelflist cards are the most efficient conversion medium, since they bibliographically mirror the item (presumably) and are compact and easily transportable. *Accession books* generally do not provide sufficient information. *Public catalogs* are usable, but include multiple cards for each item, posing a redundancy problem. Conversion can be done from the *item itself*, but this is cumbersome and requires the removal and replacement of each item.

Accession books, public catalogs, and physical items do not lend themselves to off-site conversions. Therefore, if off-site conversion is the method selected, it may be necessary to create shelflist cards or photocopy the title page and verso of each item being converted.

Libraries *migrating from systems that did not store or cannot export MARC records* may have a choice between doing another shelflist conversion or machine matching their non-MARC records. As a rule, the latter approach will be the least expensive, but will only be as successful as the amount of data in the records that can be successfully matched against a file of full MARC records.

While a keyed conversion will likely cost more per item and will require the shelflist to leave the library, a machine-matched conversion may be done in a very cost-effective manner. Keyed conversions will make use of photocopies of title page and verso if there is no shelflist or if the library cannot bear to part with its shelflist. However, photocopying

- is extremely labor intensive, and,
- will incur additional costs for supplies.

Performance measures and quality control concerns must be contractually negotiated, since there will be little direct control by the library over these. However, contracting with an outside vendor will result in predefined costs and time frames for completion. An off-site vendor conversion can therefore often be performed more efficiently with much less impact on a library's day-to-day operations.

In practice, a hybrid approach is often adopted in which all three methods are used. The bulk of the monograph collection may be sent to a vendor to be converted off-site. More difficult materials such as serials, nonprint, and local history may be converted on-site using either existing staff or contract labor, or these materials may be sent to yet another retrospective conversion vendor that specializes in converting complex, unusual items.

RETROSPECTIVE CONVERSION COSTS

The cost of a vendor-keyed or machine-matched conversion can range from approximately $0.25 to $6.00 per record and includes creation of the bibliographic database and creation of item-level holdings fields. The average cost, if the high end of the range is eliminated, is approximately $0.90 per record.

Factors affecting cost include:

- the size of the collection (per unit costs generally will be reduced as more items are converted)
- the publication dates and languages of included items (older items in foreign languages will be more expensive to convert)
- the fullness of records being provided (more information will generally make finding a matching record easier and less expensive)
- how closely local cataloging matches national standards (standard cataloging will make locating matches easier and less expensive)

Special formats such as serials and nonprint materials are more difficult to convert than monographs. Videos, foreign language materials, and older local history and genealogical titles that must be originally cataloged may cost as much as $20.00 per record. A collection sampling will provide the data needed to determine these factors and their cost implications.

The cost elements of an in-house conversion should include the cost of a database against which to convert. The most expensive options are the online bibliographic utilities such as OCLC. Less expensive are the Web- or CD-ROM-based utilities such as those offered by The Library Corporation or Marcive or Z39.50-based software such as Book Systems' *eZcat Pro*. Other costs associated with in-house conversions are equipment purchase or rental, space allocation, and personnel.

DOING A SHELFLIST ANALYSIS

Identifying, describing, and documenting existing shelflist files and the data they contain is an important preconversion activity. It enables you to determine variations in catalog card entries that can lead to inconsistencies and errors in your new machine-readable record. It also makes it possible for you to discover past and current cataloging practices that may result in a "no-match" or mismatch during retrospective conversion.

You can perform a shelflist analysis either by using a sampling method or simply by browsing through the cards in your shelflist. (For different methods, see the sources listed at the end of the chapter.) The analysis will field data for a *holdings matrix*, which will allow you to standardize entries and will serve as a guide for your ongoing cataloging efforts.

Certain areas in the collection tend to contain a high degree of catalog variation, so it probably is a good idea to start by examining the shelflist cards for these areas:

- reference
- audiovisual and any other nonprint material
- local history
- foreign language
- 910 to 920 in the Dewey call number sequence for nonfiction (The problem here is with serials that are cataloged as monographs, such as certain travel guides; in the Library of Congress system, these are found in the E and F classes.)

WHAT TO LOOK FOR

A number of cataloging practices can affect the accuracy of any potential retrospective conversion by causing a no-match or an incorrect match. These practices may be grouped into five major areas:

1. *Collection designators* (for example, "Ref," "Juv," or "Young Adult," call numbers, and main entry Cutters) are often not standardized, are inconsistently placed or used, are missing, or are simply incorrect.
2. *Serials* are often cataloged as monographs, are missing volume or part information, or are not recataloged and given separate bibliographic records when their titles change.
3. *Multiple editions* are listed on a shelflist that describes *one* edition only.

4. *Missing matching points* occur when shelflist records contain so little bibliographic information that it would be impossible to create a record for them.
5. *Miscellaneous problems:* Shelflist records are missing, illegible, misfiled, represent items that no longer exist, belong to other libraries, are ephemeral (that is, not destined for conversion), or contain possibly incomplete or inaccurate information provided by the vendors from whom libraries receive their materials preprocessed.

A checklist of other common problems can be found in Figure 13–1.

Figure 13–1 Checklist of Shelflist Problems: A Sampling

1. The shelflist contains so little bibliographic information that it will be impossible to create a record for the item.

2. There are inconsistencies in the creation of call numbers for some types of material.

3. There is little consistency or standardization in the placement of call number information on the card.

4. Title page as opposed to predominant-form cataloging is employed inconsistently for assignment of main entry.

5. Successive title cataloging for serials has not been followed, resulting in titles being changed on existing shelflists instead of being created as a new bibliographic record.

6. Title main entries have been incorrectly replaced with personal authors.

7. Author and main entry Cutters sometimes appear and sometimes do not (see number 28).

8. Titles have been changed on shelflists, but other information such as collation and imprint have been left unchanged.

9. New shelflists have not been created for different editions of a work, with the result that items are listed incorrectly on a given shelflist.

10. For titles in paperback, shelflists may reflect the bibliographic information for the hardcover edition, not the paperback.

11. Publication dates have been altered on shelflists without other data elements being edited.

12. Volume and part information is not indicated on the shelflist. (This is especially crucial for open entries.)

13. Many of the AV items and sound recordings are lacking producer names and numbers.

14. Federal documents have no shelflists and are inventoried via an accession book methodology.

15. Serials have been cataloged as monographs.

16. Pagination, LCCN, and ISBN/ISSN are missing.

17. Different editions of the same work are entered on the same shelflist.

18. Multiple copies of the same edition of a work are on different shelflists (for example, a given copy of a title is listed on both the circulating and reference shelflist with an "also in" note).

Figure 13–1 *Continued*

19. Shelflists in a given section lack that section's designator on them or contain differing abbreviations in various locations (for example, a local history section without a designator).

20. Not all foreign language materials have the language stamped or written on the shelflist.

21. Mysteries and oversized materials are shelved separately, but this is not indicated on the shelflist.

22. Many shelflist cards have been misfiled.

23. Many shelflist cards are illegible.

24. There are shelflist cards filed for items belonging to a different library.

25. Shelflists for ephemeral materials that will remain uncataloged have not been removed.

26. Information on preprocessed shelflists, such as those from Baker & Taylor and Brodart, has not been verified.

27. Nonvalidated subject headings have been assigned. (This is not critical as long as LC subject headings are accepted as they appear in the conversion records.)

28. Author Cutters sometimes appear and sometimes do not. The number of letters in the Cutter varies. (A consistent Cuttering methodology should be decided upon and implemented, and any retrospective conversion vendor should be instructed to follow that methodology regardless of what appears on the shelflist. (*This will mean that some converted records will not match spine labels exactly.*)

29. Many serial shelflists have latest and earlier edition notes, which may be difficult to reconcile with specific copy information.

30. Many juvenile shelflists include reading levels as part of the call number. (This information should be in a note field, and vendors should be instructed not to include it in the call number field. *Please note that this applies only if materials are not shelved by reading level.*)

31. Open entries tend to have individual holding years written in pencil to the right of the main entry.

32. A true union shelflist does not exist for the main building and the branches.

33. Shelflists for collections that no longer exist are still in the file. (They should be removed.)

34. Designators on the shelflist are not changed as items are moved in and out of certain collections.

Note: Those responsible for retrospective conversion should be told to ignore elements on the shelflists that have nothing to do with conversion—for example, multicolored dots, old numbers.

CREATING A HOLDINGS MATRIX

Once the shelflist has been analyzed and the problems noted, the next step is to create a holdings list that links various pieces of information into a matrix-like representation of the library's collection. This list should be composed of as many of the following elements as are applicable:

- *Library name* is a separate listing that should be created for each branch site or separate physical facility.
- *Material type* book, paperback, sound recording, film, and so on.
- *Collection indicator* is the category of material represented by the designators on the shelflist card (for example, JUV, REF, YA).
- *Location* is where items are situated in the library (for example, juvenile stacks, reference office, music room).
- *Shelflist variants* are the different designators used in the shelflist to identify a particular part of the collection.
- *Circulation category* is usually either reference or circulating.

The purpose of this list is to act as a guide in conjunction with current cataloging to assure consistency in cataloging practices, to standardize input in the creation of local holdings fields, and to be a locating device for information on the shelflist.

Once the matrix has been created, it is important to maintain it, so that it reflects any changes in cataloging practice. New materials, such as videocassettes or computer software, should have parameters established and be added to the matrix when they are added to the collection.

An example of a holdings matrix is shown in Figure 13–2.

Figure 13–2 Sample Holdings List

Branch	Media	Collection Indicator	Location	Shelflist Variants	Circulation Category
Name	1. Book 2. Paperback Book	New Jersey	Ref	1. NJ Coll B Subject's last name 2. NJ coll Call # 3. NJ coll J call #	Ref
Name	1. Book 2. Paperbook Book	Office	Front Desk	1. Office 2. Office call # 3. REF office 4. Office REF call #	Ref
Name	AV	Office	Front Desk	1. Office slides booklet 2. Office slides cassette	Circ
Name	1. Book 2. Paperback Book	Young Adult Fiction	1. Juv Stacks 2. Juv New Book	1. YA Author's last name 2. YA 1st 3 letters author's last name	Circ
Name	1. Book 2. Paperback Book	Young Adult Biography	1. Juv Stacks 2. Juv New Book	1. YAB Subject's last name 2. YA B Subject's last name	Circ
Name	AV	Game	Front Desk	Game	Circ

SOURCES

Chapman, Ann. 2000. "Revealing the Invisible: The Need for Retrospective Conversion in the Virtual Future." *Alexandria* 12, no. 1: 33–43.
This article discusses the continuing importance of retrospective conversion and examines its relevance to providing full access in a virtual setting. The author points out that titles for which no electronic record exists effectively become invisible to users. This is a particular disservice to distance learners if electronic catalogs do not include the library's complete holdings.

Chapman, Ann, Nicolas Kingsley, and Lorcan Dempsey. "Full Disclosure: Releasing the Value of Library and Archival Collections." November 3, 1999 [Online]. Available: www.ukoln.ac.uk/services/lic/fulldisclosure/. [2001, April 7].
This comprehensive eighty-page report from the United Kingdom provides an excellent history of retrospective conversion and discusses the creation and implementation of a national retrospective conversion policy in the UK. Appendices include a complete list of Web-based retrospective conversion resources subdivided by country, including many excellent sources for the United States.

Indiana University Bloomington Libraries. "Retrospective Conversion Manual." April 1, 2000 [Online]. Available: www.indiana.edu/~libtserv/staff/retro/tableofc.html [2001, April 7].
While specific to the Indiana University libraries, this online manual is an excellent model for any library's retrospective conversion processes and procedures.

Leff, Barbara. "Retrospective Conversion." December 12, 2000 [Online]. Available: www.jewishlibraries.org/ajlweb/NEWSRESOURCES_FILES/ARTSFAQS/ARTFAQ01_LEFF_RETROCON.HTM [2001, April 7].
A thorough, in-depth overview of retrospective conversion, this compilation describes the retrospective conversion process in detail including developing a plan, preparing the collection, and selecting a conversion method and vendor. This online article is especially suited to small special and school libraries.

Meernik, Mary. 1994. "Retrospective Conversion: Evolving Options, Part III." *Library Hi Tech Bibliography* no. 9: 185–204.
This bibliographic essay covers a broad range of articles written in the late 1980s and early 1990s on the subject of managing a retrospective conversion project in both the broad and narrow sense. While some articles, particularly those emphasizing the use of CD-ROM technology, are dated, many provide still useful information. Each citation includes a detailed annotation. Articles dealing with audiovisual materials, government documents,

maps, microforms, music scores, serials, and technical reports are grouped together. There is also a section on authority control management within a retrospective conversion project.

OCLC Online Computer Library Center, Inc. *Retrospective Conversion: Guidelines for Libraries.* Last update unknown [Online]. Available: www.oclc.org/oclc/promo/6075retr/6075ret1.htm [2001, April 7].
This is a comprehensive discussion of all aspects of the retrospective conversion process including planning, options, funding, getting started, and questions to ask vendors.

Schottlaender, Brian, ed. 1992. "Retrospective Conversion: History, Approaches, Considerations." *Cataloging and Classification Quarterly* 14, no. 3/4. (Issue also published as a monograph by Haworth Press in 1992.)
Three especially noteworthy articles from this issue are:

- Bolin, Mary K., and Harley B. Wright. "Retrospective Conversion of a Medium-Sized Academic Library," pp. 35–50. "This article describes methods the library used to convert its collections and examines the problems encountered with each method."

- Lentz, Edward Adrian. "Editing Recon Records: When Is Enough, Enough? A Selective Review of the Literature," pp. 129–144. Reviews issues of quality control, costs, special material formats, and collections related to editing records retrieved by bibliographic utilities.

- Maccaferri, James Tilio. "Managing Authority Control in a Retrospective Conversion Project," pp. 145–167. Considers the objectives of authority control, the degree it is needed in a retrospective conversion process, and options available to implement authority control in this context.

14 MAINTAINING THE BIBLIOGRAPHIC DATABASE

The library's bibliographic database created through a retrospective conversion will not be a static one. Titles will be added, withdrawn, transferred, and recataloged. Therefore, plans must be made for ongoing "maintenance" of the database, which can be done through your integrated, online system—assuming that the library is not a member of OCLC or some other bibliographic utility. This is why the cataloging function in your system is so important, for it is through this function that you will be able to create, add, display, edit, delete, replace, and move bibliographic as well as item records in your database.

However, there may be an interim period between when you create your machine-readable database and when your integrated system is up and running, or your current automated system may not store MARC records or allow you to maintain them. If your database is not effectively maintained, bibliographic information will become inaccurate as materials are added and deleted from your collection. Moreover, much of the value of converting holdings information as part of the retrospective conversion process may be lost, since any changes made subsequent to the conversion will not be captured.

WHAT ARE THE LIBRARY'S MAINTENANCE OPTIONS?

If a lengthy interim period is projected, your library may wish to wait to convert its local holdings information, keep paper records of title deletions and changes, and outsource the ongoing conversion of new titles. Or it may explore methodologies for loading, using, and maintaining your database online until an integrated system that provides for the storage and editing of MARC records has been selected and implemented.

The ongoing conversion of new titles can be accomplished in a variety of ways, including:

> **NOTE**
>
> A contractual arrangement for maintenance can be signed either as part of the retrospective conversion contract or separately. The costs associated with retrospective conversion may become more competitive if a vendor anticipates ongoing activity with the database. This does not preclude, however, choosing one vendor for retrospective conversion and another for ongoing maintenance.

- Catalog or contract to have materials cataloged on a bibliographic utility such as OCLC or AutoGraphics.
- Obtain MARC records from companies, such as Marcive, that specialize in providing such services to libraries.
- Use systems such as Bibliofile (Library Corporation) that provide access to the MARC files on CD-ROM for local creation of new title records.
- Use Z39.50 search software such as *BookWhere* or *eZcat* in combination with PC-based MARC editing software such as *MARC Magician* or *eZcat Pro* to find and import MARC records for editing and retention.

If your database is to be maintained at a remote location, it will be sent to the vendor or contractor with whom your library has outsourced the maintenance of its database. In the past, data was transferred mostly on magnetic tape or cartridge. While tape transfer is still used, more and more often FTP (file transfer protocol) is the method of choice for moving even large amounts of data from one computer to another over the Internet. You should forward to the vendor or contractor all additions, deletions, and changes as they occur in your collection so that the database will be continually updated and kept current.

You may wish to have local access to your database, however, in order to make it available for a service-related function, such as a public access catalog. Here, your database can be maintained in such a way that you have regular, direct access to it in one of two ways:

- A vendor hosts the database and provides you with Internet access to it.
- The database is periodically "mastered" onto disks or CD-ROMs that are accessed through a workstation or a LAN actually situated in your library. (These databases may be used later on as a backup to the online, interactive catalog.)

Additions, changes, and deletions to the database would then be handled in a variety of ways:

- Your library would directly maintain (modify) its existing holdings—over the Internet or locally through vendor-supplied software.
- New titles would be converted using one of the methods described previously.

COST FACTORS

The costs of maintaining your database after retrospective conversion will depend on the mix of maintenance options you choose. If your database, or any part of it, is maintained at a remote location, you will incur charges for the cataloging of new titles, for deletions and changes, and possibly for the storage of your database in a computer. If you maintain your existing holdings yourself, you will pay either for Internet connection charges to access the database remotely (in addition to any storage charges) or for vendor-supplied software to access the database locally (in your library).

Using your database as an offline public catalog will mean incurring additional costs, such as:

- a database setup charge
- per title charges for mastering and producing the database
- the cost of purchasing public catalog workstations
- the cost of the public catalog software
- the cost of compact disks for a CD-ROM catalog

Keeping your new machine-readable bibliographic database accurate and up to date is an essential part of automation planning and crucial to the success of your automation efforts. The system you install is only as usable as the database that supports it.

KEEPING IT RELEVANT: WEEDING YOUR COLLECTION

Materials are weeded from the library in order to maintain a current, active, and useful collection. Weeding should always be part of a library's ongoing program of collection assessment and development.

The weeding process described in this section is based on objective criteria that are simple and straightforward. But weeding involves both objective and subjective judgment: Objective criteria can provide guidelines, but they cannot replace the professional decision making.

METHODOLOGY

Begin by establishing a timeline by which the weeding of different parts of the collection needs to be completed. If you take small, defined steps, the process will seem less overwhelming. For example, you might decide that adult and juvenile fiction will be weeded by (choose a date), and adult and juvenile nonfiction will be weeded by (choose a date). At the point that you become convinced that weeding is actually doable, set deadlines for the rest of your collection. If your library is at one site, complete weeding for the entire library. If the library has a branch or two, complete it for one site.

And remember, there are no sacred cows when it comes to weeding.

Here are the steps to follow in the weeding process:

1. *Assign staff* to identify books that are eligible for weeding on the basis of any of the following criteria:
   * books published, for example, in the 1980s or earlier that have not circulated in the last five years
   * books that are *exact* duplicates of another book
   * books that are earlier editions superseded by a later edition that is on the shelf
   * books that are in poor physical condition

2. *Exceptions* to the areas to be weeded include the following:
   * all literature and literary criticism
   * all local history and archival material

WEEDING FORM

Staff (check)

_____Usage
_____Duplicate
_____Superseded
_____Condition

Librarian (check)

_____Withdraw
_____Return to shelf
_____Repair/bindery

- special collections established in commemoration of a local person or event
- anything written by a local author

3. *Procedures* for weeding:
   - Take a book truck, check-off forms (see sample form, previous page) and pencil (or pen) to stack section to be weeded, as well as system-generated reports, sorted in call number order, showing circulation activity by title.
   - Begin to scan shelves, in order, for candidates to be weeded.
   - Examine books, applying criteria for weeding.

   Note: If the system-generated report indicates that an item has not circulated in several years and the item is not on the shelf, then this fact should be noted on the system report so that the missing item can be removed from the database.

   - When a book meets any of the criteria for weeding, remove the book to the book truck and check off the reason(s) for removal on a form. Place the form in the book.
   - When finished with a section, bring books to be considered for weeding to where librarian can review them.
   - The librarian will make the final decision and indicate it on the form.
   - Books will be moved to appropriate areas of the library according to the librarian's decision. (Remember to prepare adequate storage space to hold the books removed from the shelves.)

4. *Return a book to the shelf* if there is any doubt about the wisdom of withdrawing the book, based upon:
   - known in-house use patterns (for example, sources used routinely in the library but that never circulate)
   - inherent importance of the title (for example, if the book is a classic)
   - necessary duplication (for example, multiple copies of best sellers or titles on reading lists and so on)
   - need to retain superseded edition because of its special value (for example, unique illustrations or a special introduction by a renowned authority in the earlier, original edition)

- possibility of being repaired or rebound instead of being weeded

5. *Keep accurate statistics* on the number of items actually withdrawn from the collection.

SOURCES

Baer, Nadine L., James A. Barrett, and Karl E. Johnson. 1995. "OPAC Database Creation Problems." *Information Technology and Libraries* 14, no. 3 (September): 179–184.

This article discusses the errors and data corruption that occurred when bibliographic records from five academic libraries were merged to create a union online catalog. A statistical analysis of the nature of the problems and their overall magnitude resulted in the conclusion that the creation process was flawed particularly in the area of record overlays. The lessons learned will be useful for other libraries contemplating similar cooperative projects.

Bolin, Mary K. 2000. "Catalog Design, Catalog Maintenance, Catalog Governance." *Library Collections, Acquisitions, & Technical Services* 24, no. 1: 53–63.

Bolin reviews the evolution of catalog design and maintenance from the typed catalog card to the Web catalog of the present day. She points out that design and maintenance of the catalog together equal catalog governance or professional responsibility for the catalog. The article discusses how design and maintenance methods have become more numerous and varied as the catalog has evolved from a card to an electronic entity and explores how standards are still the foundation of the catalog even though its format may be much more varied and customized.

Evans, G. Edward. 2000. *Developing Library and Information Center Collections*. 4th ed. Englewood, Colo.: Libraries Unlimited.

Chapter 14, "Deselection," defines deselection, or weeding; describes its uses by different types of libraries, reasons and barriers, and criteria for deselection; and ends with a useful list of further readings of general materials and sources listed by library type (academic, public, school, and special).

Klopfer, Karen. "Weed It! For an Attractive and Useful Collection." November 21, 2000 [Online]. Available: www.wmrls.org/resources/weeding.html [2001, March 6].

This Web site discusses why we need to weed, public relations issues involving the library's public, "Are Some Materials Sacred?" disposing of weeded materials, and convincing staff and the public that weeding is necessary.

Kulczak, Deb, and Lora L. Lennertz. 1999. "Smart and Smarter: How to Raise the IQ of Your Barcodes." *College & Undergraduate Libraries* 6, no.1: 81–94.
This article addresses the database cleanup required after a smart bar-coding project with specific descriptions of the problems encountered and strategies for problem resolution.

Livingston, Sally. "Weeding Library Media Center Collections." 1997 [Online]. Available: www.pld.fayette.k12.ky.us/lms/html/weed.htm [2001, March 6]. This document presents "words of wisdom" about weeding based on personal experience, a survey of the literature, and the Jefferson County Public Schools weeding manual. It includes a discussion of skills librarians need in order to weed, procedures for weeding, collection mapping, and discarding procedures.

Slote, Stanley J. 1997. *Weeding Library Collections: Library Weeding Methods*. 4th ed. Englewood, Colo.: Libraries Unlimited.
This book was first published in 1975. The author shows how to identify the core collections versus the weedable collections and discusses a variety of traditional and computer-assisted methods for weeding. This is a practical guide that outlines step-by-step procedures.

Stankowski, Rebecca House. 1990. "Bibliographic Record Maintenance and Control in a Consortium Database." *Cataloging and Classification Quarterly* 12, no. 2: 47–62.
This article approaches bibliographic database maintenance from the perspective of a multitype library consortium. It discusses in detail the difficulties that occur when the quality of records in a cooperative database vary widely and proposes methods of dealing with problems of joint input and database maintenance.

15 BAR CODING YOUR COLLECTION

Almost everyone is familiar with the zebra-striped labels that have become ubiquitous in our lives, from the supermarket line to the materials that we buy for our libraries. Bar codes owe their success to the design that allows unique information to be programmed into their stripes and then read accurately and quickly by readers and scanners attached to computers.

Bar codes have become an indispensable part of library automation because they serve as a computerized accession number—a unique identifier that links a specific book, journal, compact disk, and the like—to the computerized bibliographic record that describes it.

WHAT IS BAR CODING?

Bar coding attaches a bar-code label to an item in the library's collection or to a borrower's library card. There are several ways to bar code the items associated with your materials files, borrower files, and other files that you must link to the correct electronic records in your bibliographic, borrower, and other appropriate databases.

SMART BAR CODES

One popular method for labeling and linking the collection utilizes customized, or smart, bar codes. Smart bar codes are created by means of computerized processing of the item information already contained in the bibliographic record. The item information is then linked to a unique number and a corresponding bar-code label is printed that, as suggested below, includes a mix of eye-readable matching points such as call number, location, truncated author or title, publication date, and edition.

YOUR LIBRARY NAME (35)
CALL NUMBER (40)   Location (9)
Title of this book (40 positions)
Author's Name (40)

3 1234 56789004 9

You should consider this method if your collection has already been retrospectively converted and contains the information necessary to create the item record through machine processing. It will be most successful if item information has been entered consistently, if call numbers are unique, and if database maintenance is up to date so that bar codes are not created for items that, for example, have been withdrawn from the collection. Libraries using the Dewey Decimal Classification can still use smart bar codes as long as enough eye-readable information is printed on the bar-code label to identify the item clearly.

Smart bar codes cost more than generic bar codes initially both for production of the labels and for the machine processing required to support their use. Common problems in smart bar-coding projects include:

- items for which no label has been printed—principally duplicate copies, multivolume sets, and items for which there was no information in the database
- bar-code labels created for nonexistent items
- bar codes created with insufficient identifying information to match them with the item on the shelf

Because a smart bar code has already been attached to an item in the automated system, any human error that results in attaching the bar-code label to the wrong item will have negative implications.

Smart bar codes do have advantages, however:

- Materials do not have to be physically transported to workstations to be linked.
- The bar-coding and linking process can be completed in one step, saving personnel costs.
- There is little "on-the-fly" conversion to deal with at the circulation desk.

It is less important to attach an eye-readable bar-code number to the shelflist, particularly if the shelflist is to be closed following the completion of the automation project. However, if the shelflist is being maintained, it is helpful to attach a label that is both eye- and machine-readable.

GENERIC BAR CODES

For those libraries that have not completed retrospective conversion or that do not have sufficient item information in their bibliographic records to make the use of smart bar codes practical, the use of generic, or "dumb," bar codes may be the best approach. Dumb bar codes have no inherent connection to an item and basically consist of a bar code and an eye-readable number that can be attached randomly to materials in the collection.

YOUR LIBRARY NAME

3 5492 09387016 4

There are two ways to utilize dumb bar codes:

1. Take the items to be bar coded and linked to a terminal, bar code each item, then link the item into the system by matching it with the appropriate bibliographic record, transferring necessary item information, and wanding, scanning, or keying the bar-code number to complete the process. (Note: It is often useful to have the shelflist available, since all of the necessary information may not be available or readily visible on the piece itself.)
2. Take the shelflist to the shelves, bar code both the item and the shelflist, then link the item into the system from the shelflist.

Items can also be linked "on-the-fly" at the circulation desk using dumb bar codes.

The disadvantages to this method are apparent. Either all items in the collection must be moved to and from workstations, or a two-step process of labeling and linking must be adopted. This involves taking the shelflist drawers out to the stacks, which takes longer and requires more human labor.

However, dumb bar codes are less expensive than smart bar codes, and there are no machine-processing costs incurred. It is also less likely that items will be mislinked, since the bar codes have not been preassigned to a specific bibliographic record.

Some prefer on-the-fly conversion since only those items in the collection that are being used are initially bar coded. However, this method can cause congestion at the circulation desk and, with the proliferation of online catalogs, can prevent items from being used simply because they have not been linked and are therefore not accessible through the OPAC.

Often combining both dumb and smart bar codes results in the most successful projects. Smart bar codes can be used most effectively with monographs, while serials, continuations, and multivolume sets are better labeled and linked using dumb bar codes.

Dumb bar codes are generally used for linking borrowers to a database because preloading of borrower information is not as widespread as preloading of item information. In some cases, registration or personnel tapes may be available so that borrower information can also be processed using smart bar codes.

GETTING BAR CODES

Bar codes may be purchased as singles (one zebra stripe and eye-readable label), doubles (one zebra stripe and two eye-readable labels), duplicates (two zebra stripes and eye-readable labels), or triplicates (three zebra stripes and eye-readable labels). When using dumb bar codes, it is wise to put at least an eye-readable bar-code number on the shelflist and borrower registration forms during an initial conversion. Later, if paper files are dispensed with, a single combination bar-code and eye-readable number can be used.

There are several bar-code formats available. The ones most used by library automation systems have fourteen-digit numbers using either the Codabar or Code 39, also known as Code 3 of 9, designs. These bar-code labels have the following structure:

Digit:	1	2 3 4 5	6 7 8 9 10 11 12 13	14
Meaning:	Item Type	Institution Number	Item or Patron Identification Number	Check Digit

This structure may be described further as follows:

ITEM TYPE: Distinguishes materials from patrons.

INSTITUTION NUMBER: A four-digit number representing the library (institution) whose bar code this is. Use either your institution's OCLC Name Address Control Number (NACN) or some other code specific to your library such as a portion of the phone number or the last four digits of the extended zip code. Alternatively, the retrospective conversion or local system vendor may assign an arbitrarily designated number.

ITEM OR PATRON IDENTIFICATION NUMBER: This is a sequentially-assigned, eight-digit number representing the items in a library's collection. Begin numbering with 00000001.

CHECK DIGIT: This is a modulus–10, type–1 check digit, which is calculated using the values of digits 1–13.

BAR CODING BEFORE BUYING A SYSTEM

It is possible to bar code a collection prior to selecting a system, and it can be particularly efficient to do so during an inventory process. If you choose to do this, remember that:

- You must choose one of the two standard formats.
- You need to include the standard number of digits, including a check digit.
- Item labels must be numerically distinguishable from borrower labels.

If you go this route, you must attend scrupulously to database maintenance during the interim period. This can be time consuming and difficult if the database cannot be easily accessed. Dumb bar codes are probably the better choice in cases such as this, particularly if the lag time between labeling and system implementation will be more than just a few months. Regardless of the type of bar code chosen, it is highly desirable to attach a bar code to the shelflist if labeling is done prior to system selection.

It is advisable, for purposes of durability, to purchase labels with a laminate coating, although these are slightly more expensive. It is also important to include the name of the library on the label bearing the zebra-stripe coding along with the eye-readable identifier, as shown in the examples.

Before beginning to bar code, you must decide where on the item the bar code will be placed. There are several possibilities.

One is to put the bar code in the upper left-hand corner of the outside front cover of a book. This allows easy accessibility during charge-out and check-in and, for inventory purposes, allows the label to be seen easily when the item is on the shelf. Labels may be placed vertically or horizontally, with the position determined by what the staff consider to be easiest to wand and scan.

If duplicate or triplicate bar codes are used, one can be placed on the outside of the book and another in a more protected location inside the item. The costs associated with duplicate and triplicate labels, however, are significantly higher than those for single or double labels.

The bar code can also be placed inside the book near the book pocket, particularly if the book must be opened anyway to insert a date due card.

Libraries with round-the-clock access, but lacking round-the-clock staffing, may wish to place one bar-code label on the book and one on the book card itself, so that books can be charged easily when staff return. Libraries located in hospitals and corporations may fall into this category.

Finally, labeling more exotic items such as compact disks, filmstrips, toys, and equipment require more creative placement schemes. Often in these cases, the labels end up on the packaging, rather than on the piece itself.

BAR-CODING ISSUES IN SYSTEM MIGRATION

Libraries migrating from legacy systems often have a plethora of bar-coding challenges confronting them. One of the most common problems is that the library originally selected bar codes that had far fewer than fourteen digits, were neither Codabar nor Code 3 of 9, and employed no check digit. If the library's database must be retrospectively converted again as well, it is possible to correct the bar-code anomalies by including the generation of smart bar codes as part of the retrospective conversion project. Even if the database is satisfactory, a smart bar-code project may still be a more cost-effective means of replacing existing bar codes than relinking the entire collection item by item. No matter what, though, manually attaching the new bar-code labels, whether smart or dumb, to each item, cannot be avoided.

THINKING ABOUT OTHER BAR-CODING ISSUES

A separate issue from system conversion is the issue of older bar codes that meet standards but were placed inside books when the library first automated. Most new systems provide for laser scanners that can easily read a bar code on the front or back cover, so materials can be quickly "swiped" through the reader, allowing circulation desk staff to charge and discharge materials more quickly and easily without having to open each book.

A process known as "bar cloning" now allows staff to scan the old bar-code label and to have a matching bar code instantly printed that can then be applied to the exterior of the book or other item.

It is particularly effective when the circulation desk is configured so that the charging unit and security sensitizer are laid out to allow staff to be able to scan the item through the charging unit and across the desensitizer in one motion. This configuration will save hundreds of hours a year in a busy library, freeing circulation staff to assist users in other ways.

ORGANIZING THE BAR-CODING PROJECT

Placing bar codes on materials can be done in-house by staff or volunteers, or the project may be outsourced. If multiple bar codes are being placed on materials, shelflists, and book cards, working in teams of two helps ensure that duplicate or triplicate pairs are not mismatched. Written instructions (see Figure 15–1) make the project easier for everyone, especially if you use volunteers or contract labor.

Figure 15–1 Instructions for a Bar-Coding Project

WHAT TEAMS OF TWO PEOPLE WILL NEED

- Book truck
- Pencils
- Scrap cards
- Shelflist drawer
- Sheets of item bar-code labels

PLACEMENT OF BAR CODES ON SHELFLIST CARDS

1. Get a shelflist drawer.

2. Put a 3x5 card with the team names in the front of the drawer, leaving room for more writing on the card.

3. Remove the rod from the shelflist drawer.

4. Go to the shelf position for the first item in the shelflist drawer or to the place where the last work was done on the project. You will work from the shelf to the shelflist drawer.

5. One person will read aloud from the spine the call number and title of an item. The second person will locate the shelflist card and bar-code labels. **Note:** Smart bar-code labels will have call numbers and titles printed on the labels.

6. The bar-code labels come in matched pairs. Be certain that you are using the *matched pair*.

7. When you have a matching physical item and shelflist card, attach a bar-code label to the physical item.

8. Put the companion bar-code label on the back of the shelflist card. Note: If there is a third label, it may be put inside the item or on the book card.

9. For multivolume or multicopy books:
   a. Put the bar code on the shelflist, making sure the volume-identifying information is clearly matched to the bar-code number.
   b. Make new bar-code cards if all of the volumes or copies will not fit on the existing shelflist cards.
   c. When you must start new cards for serials or items with multiple volumes, use a *blank* card with the following information:
      i. format (if other than book)
      ii. call number
      iii. title; after the title, put "bar-code card #2," or whatever card number this will be.
   d. Begin placing the bar codes in a column starting in the lower left-hand corner of the

Figure 15–1 *Continued*

shelflist and continuing up the side. Begin the second column at the bottom of the shelflist. Leave space at the side for volume or year information.

e.   Because of card width, do not put more than two columns of bar codes on a card.

f.   Put bar codes on both sides of the card.

g.   When all volumes are done, you may staple the shelflist cards together, if practical.

10.   Return the shelflist card to the drawer and the item to the shelf.

11.   Continue to the next item on the shelf.

12.   Stand up any shelflists for which there is no item on the shelf.

13.   If you stop work before you finish a drawer, note on the 3x5 card in the front of the drawer where you left off and the date.

14.   When a drawer is completed, write "bar coded," the date completed, and the team members' names on the 3x5 card.

PLACEMENT OF BAR CODES ON PACKAGING MATERIALS

15.   Attach the bar-code label, when possible, to the outside upper left-hand corner of the front cover of items.

16.   Try not to cover information that may be on the cover of the item.

17.   If there is a very loose transparent cover on the item, put the bar code *under* the plastic, directly on the item. If there is no room to put the bar code under the plastic, put it *on* the plastic.

18.   Press the labels firmly to be sure they will stick.

19.   On compact disk cases: Put the bar-code label in the upper right-hand corner.

20.   On other nonprint materials (for example, slides, filmstrips)

a.   Determine the upper left-hand corner of most boxes by positioning the box so that the edge title label is read as a book spine, with the box standing on its bottom edge, the top opening to the right.

b.   With boxes that have removable (not hinged) bottoms (usually filmstrips and slides), put the bar-code label on the lid.

SOURCES

Gatten, Jeffrey N. 1990. "Bar Coding Projects: Preparation and Execution." *Library Hi Tech* 8, no. 1 (Issue 29): 21–27.
"This article attempts to provide a comprehensive overview of the relevant issues for a successful bar-coding project. Selecting bar codes, planning and structuring a project, calculating time estimates, and maintaining staff morale are presented in detail. A selected bibliography provides access to more information."

Kulczak, Deb, and Lora L. Lennertz. 1999. "Smart and Smarter: How to Raise the IQ of Your Barcodes." *College & Undergraduate Libraries* 6, no. 1: 81–94.
The authors discuss in detail the planning and implementation of a smart bar-coding project at the University of Arkansas. They emphasize that the problems associated with bar coding are the same regardless of the size of the library's collection and provide detailed information on procedures, process evaluation, and lessons learned.

Leslie, Donald S. 1995. "Barcodes: The Cornerstone of Materials Flow Management." *Computers in Libraries*, 15, no. 3 (March): 30–32.
"This article explores the role of bar codes in materials flow management and particularly how bar codes contribute to productivity in the library. In addition, it provides case studies on libraries that have rebarcoded their collections to allow them to make the best use of the technology now available, therefore improving patron satisfaction and employee performance."

16 APPLYING THE MARC STANDARD

If you are going to automate your library, then paper files (such as the card catalog), the shelflist, authority files, and community information referral files must be in a form that a computer can read. When these files are laid out in a *standardized* manner, they become machine-readable—that is, comprehensible to a computer.

MARC, short for MAchine Readable Cataloging, constitutes a group of communications formats that conforms to the American National Standard for Bibliographic Information Interchange (NISO Z39.2). It is the vehicle for converting bibliographic paper files to machine-readable ones.

WHAT IS MARC—MACHINE READABLE CATALOGING?

MARC was originally developed by the Library of Congress in the 1960s as a means of translating the information on catalog cards into a format that could be read, stored, and processed by a computer. Initially known as the "LC MARC" format, it is now referred to as USMARC, although the two terms are often used interchangeably. In 1997 the Library of Congress and the National Library of Canada merged the USMARC and CANMARC formats to create MARC 21. The transition from USMARC was completed in 2000. MARC 21, however, is not radically different from its predecessor since it follows the Library of Congress's commitment to maintain MARC as a stable format accompanied by gradual change.

In the MARC format, each discrete title, often equivalent to a shelflist card, becomes a bibliographic record. Similarly, each card in an authority file, including the cross-reference cards in the catalog, becomes an authority record. Cards in referral files become community information records.

Here are some basics about the layout of a MARC record:

- *Fields:* Each item of information—personal, corporate, or meeting name; title; imprint; facility; program; subject; and so on—is assigned its own special place, called a field, within the MARC record. Each field must have an address or label that tells the computer what kind of information the field contains. Using full words like "title" and "subject" takes up too much storage space within the computer, so three-digit numbers called *tags* replace these descriptive terms. Using digits also guarantees that fields are called the same thing every time.

For example:

–100 tag marks the personal name field
–245 tag marks the title information field
–856 tag marks the electronic location and access field

Figure 16–1 offers a list of some commonly used MARC fields.

- *Subfields:* Sometimes the information within a field must be broken down further. For example, the "electronic location and access" field includes the name of the electronic host, its location, and the Uniform Resource Locator (URL) World Wide Web address. Each piece of information must be preceded by the equivalent of an apartment number in order for the (dumb) computer to understand where one ends and another begins.

  To conserve space, the descriptive terms are replaced by single lower-case letters called *subfield codes*, which are preceded by a special character called a *subfield delimiter* (–). Because many keyboards cannot create the delimiter, other special characters, such as an underline (_) or a dollar sign ($) may be used. The subfield codes are standardized so that the same ones always appear to define a specific piece of information within a given field.

  Field tags may also be followed by one or two single-digit *indicators*, which represent values that interpret or supplement the data found in the field. Each indicator has its own discrete meaning. In the following example, the "1" represents the need for a separate title entry in the catalog and the "4" represents the number of nonfiling characters at the beginning of the field:

24514$a The American heritage guide to antiques /$cMary Durant.

Tags, subfield codes, and indicators together are referred to as *content designators*. They describe the contents of the fields in terms that a computer can understand. Records that include these content designators are referred to as *tagged records*.

- Each tagged record also has a *leader* and a *directory*. The leader is the first 24 characters of the record and contains programming information for the computer. The directory tells what tags are in the record and describes their placement. The directory is necessary because the MARC Communications Format formats the record into a long continuous string of fields with no tags. The directory explains to the computer how to reformat the record, after its transfer, into usable fields of data.
- The last important segment of a MARC bibliographic record is the *008 field*, Fixed-Length Data Elements, also known as "Fixed Field Codes." It provides such information as whether the item being described in the record is a monograph or serial, what country it was published in, the subject heading system for an authority record, facilities availability for a community information record, and its frequency (if it is a serial).

Figure 16–1 Some Commonly Used MARC Fields

001 Control number

005 Date and time of latest transaction

008 Fixed-length data elements (date entered, publication status, place of publication, language, modified record, cataloging source)

010 LC control number

100 Main Entry—personal name

110 Main Entry —corporate name

245 Title statement

250 Edition statement

260 Publication, distribution, etc. (imprint)

300 Physical description

400 Series Statement /added entry—personal name

440 Series Statement /added entry—title

500 General note

520 Summary, abstract, annotation, scope, etc. note

600 Subject added entry—personal name

650 Subject added entry—topical term

651 Subject added entry—geographic name

700 Added entry—personal name

710 Added entry—corporate name

UNDERSTANDING WHY MARC IS SO IMPORTANT

The most time-consuming and perhaps most expensive activity that you will undertake to automate your library is converting your manual files to machine-readable ones. For your bibliographic files, you will want to do it only once—trust us on this. This means that you must convert your files using a standard that can be read and used by most library automation systems so that your bibliographic database will be transportable when you decide to trade in your existing system for a new one.

This transportability is becoming even more important as more and more libraries have begun to migrate to different systems. Those libraries with bibliographic databases in full MARC format have a relatively easy time extracting their records from the old system and loading them into the new one. This is not the case for libraries with bibliographic records that do not conform to the MARC format. For these libraries, it often costs thousands of dollars to reformat their records and sometimes they are faced with yet another retrospective conversion project. It pays to do it right the first time. Moreover, a database of full MARC records ensures the availability of the most complete records available, so that your public will have the best access possible to all of the information resources you are making available.

The only way to achieve these goals is to make sure that your records are in MARC 21 format. These records are available from a number of bibliographic utilities and vendors either online or on CD-ROM. Several book jobbers will provide a MARC record for a small charge for books you purchase from them. The important thing to remember at this point is to settle for nothing less than full-length, MARC 21 bibliographic records.

DISCOVERING THAT MARC CAN'T DO IT ALL: NEW ELEMENTS OF DESCRIPTION

For many years, the MARC formats seemed to be all that a library needed to effectively describe its resources. That changed with the advent of the World Wide Web and the general availability of information resources and data that moved far beyond the realm of bibliographic descriptors contained on a 3x5 catalog card. MARC remains the gold standard for traditional bibliographic data. It will not be going away anytime soon, but it is not well-suited for the description of electronic resource content or archival finding aids.

The organization of electronic and Internet resources—"cataloging the Web," if you will—is becoming increasingly more important. Initially, cataloging Internet and other electronic resources was done utilizing traditional forms of bibliographic description found in MARC and AACR2. However, for these ever more important electronic and Internet resources, new elements of description are being devised that may soon become either de facto or formalized standards.

(**Note:** MARC, AACR2, and other such descriptors are sometimes known as "metadata," that is, data about data, or, information that makes it possible to find, access, use, and manage information resources.)

The Dublin Core Metadata Initiative, started by OCLC and the National Center for Supercomputing Applications (NCSA) in a series of workshops beginning in the mid–1990s, is an effort to develop a core set of semantics for Web-based resources in order to categorize the Web for easier search and retrieval. The efforts of the working groups involved in this project to adopt a common core of semantics for electronic resource description have resulted in a draft standard—Z39.85–200x, the Dublin Core Metadata Element Set. This draft standard, created by a cross-disciplinary, international group, may soon be the first standard approved by the U.S. National Information Standards Organization (NISO) under its new "Fast Track" approval process.

While the Dublin Core metadata vocabulary originally focused on describing digital and Web-based resources, its focus and purpose have broadened considerably so that it is now able to provide descriptive information about any kind of resource regardless of its format or medium. The OpenURL standard, currently in development, will extend this concept by providing a standardized syntax for describing Web-transportable packages of bibliographic metadata and identifiers about information objects between the systems of different information providers. A NISO committee will be charged with building the syntax that will define the new standard.

Two other specifications, the Encoded Archival Description Document Type Definition (EAD DTD) and the Text Encoding and Interchange Document Type Definition (TEI DTD), are nonproprietary Standard Generalized Markup Language (SGML) encoding standards for machine-readable finding aids and electronic texts created by archives, libraries, and museums. The EAD DTD is maintained by the MARC Standards Office in the Library of Congress and the Society of American Archivists. The TEI DTD is hosted by four international universities and sponsored by the Text Encoding Initiative consortium consisting of the Association for Computers and the Humanities, the Association for Computational Linguistics, and the Association for Literary and Linguistic Computing.

Both EAD and TEI developed, as did the Dublin Core, in the 1990s. The EAD specification is closely connected to the MARC 21 format, while the TEI specification complements rather than mirrors it. It is possible that the Dublin Core Metadata set will in time absorb these two specifications, especially if it becomes a formalized NISO standard.

Clearly MARC can't do it all. However, as the grandparent of bibliographic machine-readable standards, it has paved the way for Dublin Core and other document type definitions. Its importance cannot be underestimated, even as these new standards join it in describing and sharing data and information about the many resources now available to all of us.

CONCLUSION

This has been a very brief introduction to MARC and some other important standards of description for information resources. For those wishing to delve further into their mysteries, see the list of sources.

Following the MARC standard, though, is like following the Yellow Brick Road. You stray from it at your peril, substantially risking your chances of getting to the Emerald City—that is, to a successful automation project—without expensive, sometimes fatal, encounters with the Wicked Witch of Bibliographic Incompatibility.

SOURCES

Byrne, Deborah J. 1998. *MARC Manual: Understanding and Using MARC Records.* 2d ed. Englewood, Colo.: Libraries Unlimited.
All three types of MARC records—bibliographic, authority, and holdings—are explained, along with specifications for MARC database processing, MARC products, and online systems. The second edition includes a new chapter on MARC format integration and updates all information, including that on MARC authority records and holdings records.

Cataloger's Desktop. Washington, D.C.: Cataloging Distribution Service, Library of Congress, quarterly subscription.
Current contents on one CD-ROM, updated quarterly, include:
- Anglo-American Cataloguing Rules (AACR2) with Amendments 1999
- Archives, Personal Papers and Manuscripts: A Cataloging Manual
- Library of Congress Rule Interpretations
- Subject Cataloging Manuals
- MARC 21 formats for Bibliographic Data, Authority Data, Holdings Data, Classification Data, Community Information
- Latest editions of all five MARC Code Lists
- Archival Moving Image Materials: A Cataloging Manual
- CONSER (serials) Cataloging Manual and CONSER Editing Guide
- Graphic Materials: Rules for Describing Original Items and Historical Collections
- Map Cataloging Manual
- Music Cataloging Decisions
- Rare Book cataloging tools
- Thesaurus for Graphic Materials
- Descriptive Cataloging Manual
- LC Cutter Table
- Library of Congress Filing Rules

"Dublin Core Metadata Initiative." Last update unknown [Online]. Available: http://dublincore.org/ [2001, April 7].
This Web site gives an overview of the Dublin Core Metadata Initiative (DCMI), the Dublin Core Element Set and Qualifiers, a usage guide, and information on the DCMI working and interest groups.

Fritz, Deborah A. 1998. *Cataloging with AACR2 and USMARC for Books, Computer Files, Serials, Sound Recordings, Videorecordings.* Chicago: American Library Association.
Although not yet updated to reflect MARC 21, this easy-to-use guide is still a useful manual. "Organized in a format similar to AACR2—according to major media types—the guide provides searching hints, match criteria, the relationships between fields in the cataloging record, ISBD punctuation, and much more." The loose-leaf format facilitates updating.

Furrie, Betty. 2000. *Understanding MARC Bibliographic: Machine-Readable Cataloging*. 5th ed. Washington, D.C.: Cataloging Distribution Service, Library of Congress, in collaboration with The Follett Software Company. "This booklet will explain—in the simplest terms possible—what a MARC record is, and it will provide the basic information needed to understand and evaluate a MARC record." Also available in a Web edition: November 2000—last update [Online]. Available: www.loc.gov/marc/umb/ [2001, April 7].

Library of Congress, Network Development and MARC Standards Office. MARC Standards. March 13, 2000 [Online]. Available: http://lcweb.loc.gov/marc/ [2001, April 7].
MARC documentation, development, concise formats, code lists, and other essential information are available on this Web site. Also included is information on MARC SGML and XML and MARC records, systems, and tools.

Miller, Steven J., comp. "Metadata and Cataloging Internet Resources: Selected Articles, Reference Documents, and Web Sites." Updated May 2000 [Online]. Available: www.uwm.edu/~mll/resource.html [2001, May 30].
This is an extensive bibliography composed of both print and online articles and resources. A link to the current syllabus of the author's Metadata and Internet Cataloging course syllabus provides access to additional current resources.

Milstead, Jessica, and Susan Feldman. "Metadata: Cataloging By Any Other Name . . . " January 1999 [Online]. Available: www.onlineinc.com/onlinemag/OL1999/milstead1.html [2001, May 30].
The authors discuss the concept of metadata and its importance to both authors and users of electronic information. They point out that catalogers and indexers have been standardizing metadata for centuries in order to organize information effectively. A companion piece on "Metadata Projects and Standards" along with an extensive selection of resource links accompany the article. The authors succeed in demonstrating the relationships and commonalities between traditional cataloging and indexing tools and the newer metadata content and encoding concepts currently being developed to describe and catalog electronic information.

Olson, Nancy B., ed. *Cataloging Internet Resources: A Manual and Practical Guide*. 2d ed. Dublin, Ohio: OCLC Online Computer Library Center, Inc., 1997 [Online]. Available: www.purl.org/oclc/cataloging-internet [2001, May 30].
This manual provides detailed instructions for cataloging Internet resources using traditional tools and standards of bibliographic description, including MARC and AACR2. There is some discussion of the issues involved in having bibliographic records for Internet resources not locally owned in a catalog and how that affects item information and displays when the records never have local holdings attached to them.

17 LEARNING ABOUT OTHER STANDARDS

WHAT OTHER STANDARDS ARE IMPORTANT TO LIBRARIES?

Any library undertaking an automation project should adhere to standards. Standards are sets of specifications that, when conformed to, result in interchangeability and portability of files and networking architectures from one system to another.

Standards allow different systems to interface with one another. There are recognized standards for:

- bibliographic data and formats
- item formats
- transaction formats
- cabling and networking of hardware
- information transfer
- textual data files
- image and multimedia files
- CD-ROM files
- e-books

Standards must be proposed to and approved by a national or international standards organization. These organizations include the

- International Standards Organization (ISO)
- National Information Standards Organization (NISO [Z39])*
- American National Standards Institute (ANSI)
- Institute of Electrical and Electronics Engineers (IEEE)
- Telecommunications Industries Association (TIA)

---

* The National Information Standards Organization is a not-for-profit corporation accredited by the American National Standards Institute (ANSI) that develops, maintains, and publishes technical standards used by libraries, information services, and publishers. The standards cited in this book are available in print and CD-ROM formats for purchase and online for free download as PDF files *(www.niso.org)*.

- Internet Engineering Task Force (IETF)
- Electronic Industry Association (EIA)

Some widely adopted documents such as AACR2 and the ALA character set are not standards in the strict sense because they have not been specifically adopted by a recognized standards organization. They have achieved such a high level of acceptance, however, that they are considered de facto standards.

Some standards, particularly those for bibliographic formats, must be implemented by the library prior to the selection and implementation of a system. Others must be required of vendors through an RFP as part of the procurement process. This chapter provides an overview of specific standards and why they are important.

COMPREHENDING BIBLIOGRAPHIC FORMAT AND DATA ELEMENT STANDARDS

Standards for the format and description of bibliographic information in a machine-readable database are important for a number of reasons:

- These standards are well-established and accepted. They are supported by the major bibliographic utilities (for example, OCLC/WLN) and the majority of North American libraries.
- They are critical if libraries are to maintain the portability of their files. Without standards, files cannot easily be transferred from one automated system to another without engaging in a costly, repeat retrospective conversion project.
- Libraries wishing to participate in resource-sharing arrangements with other libraries will find adherence to the standards a condition of participation.

To comply with the standards for formatting and describing bibliographic information, libraries must:

- Use AACR2 Revised, all full MARC formats for bibliographic and authority data, and the International Standard Bibliographic Description (ISBD). The MARC communications formats (see Chapter 16) are based on the Information Exchange Format standard (NISO Z39.2–1994/ISO 2709).

- Establish and include in a machine-readable record all critical bibliographic data elements—for example, main entry, title, subtitle, statement of responsibility, edition, and imprint.
- Verify and include data elements unique to the item. These include:
  1. LCCN (Library of Congress Catalog Number)
  2. ISBN (International Standard Book Number, ISO 2108)
  3. ISSN (International Standard Serial Number, ISO 3297)
  4. SICI (Serial Item and Contribution Identifier, Z39.56)
- Require support for:
  1. the American Library Association's Extended ASCII Character Set for Romanized Languages, which is generally the same as NISO Z39.47, ANSEL (Extended Latin Alphabet Coded Character Set for Bibliographic Use)
  2. Unicode (ISO 10646) for non-Romanized languages
- Establish local policy on the treatment of certain bibliographic data elements. For example, should preference be given to the information provided online or to local information (such as local subject headings or notes)? A library might accept without change the record for a straight fiction title, but may wish to make changes in the record for a local history title.
- Establish a hierarchy of acceptance when confronted with multiple full MARC machine-readable records (such as those of the Library of Congress, National Library of Medicine, or local libraries) for the same bibliographic item.

UNDERSTANDING ITEM FORMAT STANDARDS

Formatting standards and designated fields within the MARC record accommodate the information required to locate and identify an item and enumerate holdings. In 1999 the "Holdings Statements for Bibliographic Items (NISO Z39.71)" combined and replaced the previous item standards:

- Serials Holding Statements (NISO Z39.44)
- Holdings Statements for Non-Serial Items (NISO Z39.57)

To properly implement item format standards, libraries must document both current and past entry practices and establish consistent forms of entry for current cataloging. When standardizing item information locally, libraries must:

- Decide on the treatment of and include all critical data elements that provide inventory information on each physical item, including holding library, holding branch, internal location, prefix (Ref, J, and so on), classification number, Cutter number, volume data, and serial patterns, enumeration, and chronology.
- Include a unique item identifier (that is, a bar-code number).
- Normalize or standardize inconsistent collection codes and other local designators. (See Chapter 13 for tips on preparing your shelflist for conversion.)

UNDERSTANDING TRANSACTION FORMAT STANDARDS

The Circulation Interchange Protocol (NCIP; ANSI/NISO Z39.83–200x) will support reciprocal borrowing and interlibrary loan transactions among library systems. It will facilitate direct-patron borrowing, remote-patron authentication, and controlled access to electronic documents. This standard, currently a Draft Standard for Trial Use, replaces Patron Record Data Elements (NISO Z39.69) and Format for Circulation Transactions (NISO Z39.70).

The potential exists for this protocol to facilitate the migration of patron and circulation transaction files from one local system to another. However, there is less vendor interest in this level of transportability than in the ability to share more limited data for purposes of facilitating reciprocal borrowing and interlibrary loan.

INTERPRETING STANDARDS FOR THE CABLING AND NETWORKING OF HARDWARE

As we have discussed earlier in this book, automated library systems now run on networks—local area networks (LANs) and wide area networks (WANs) or metropolitan area networks (MANs)—comprised of personal computers used as servers and workstations. As a result, libraries must be aware of cabling, network, and telecommunications standards when implementing networks within the library so that existing networks will be compatible with the integrated library systems now on the market.

Some of the major standards are:

- Commercial Building Telecommunications Cabling Standard (EIA/TIA–568A)
- Telecommunications & Information Exchange Between Systems—LANs and MANs (IEEE 802)
- Wireless Telecommunications & Information Exchange (IEEE802.1b)
- Telecommunications & Information Exchange Between Systems (CSMA/CD) (Ethernet) (IEEE 802.3/ISO 8802.3)
- Frame Relay (ANSI T1–617–618)
- Asynchronous Transfer Mode (ITU ATM)
- Interface Between Data Terminal Equipment and Data Communication Equipment (EIA RS–232-C–69)
- Small Computer System Interface (SCSI) (ANSI ASC x3.268)

UNDERSTANDING INFORMATION TRANSFER STANDARDS

The ability of integrated library systems to interface and interact electronically with one another and with other external information resources is now one of the highest priorities of libraries planning for automation. Successful implementation of these linkages requires adherence to standards and protocols that allow disparate systems to "talk" electronically with each other. These include:

- American Standard Code for Information Exchange (ASCII) (ANSI X3.4)
- Interlibrary Loan Service Definition and Protocol (ISO OSI 10160–10161)
- Open Systems Interconnection (OSI) Reference Model (ISO 7498)
- Hypertext Transfer Protocol (HTTP) (W3C RFC 2626)
- Transmission Control Protocol/Internet Protocol (ANSI TCP/IP)
- Portable Operating System Interface (POSIX) (IEEE 1003.1/ ISO 9945)
- Standards for Programming Languages (ANSI ASC X3)
- Information Retrieval Application Service Definition and Protocol Specification for Open System (NISO Z39.50/ISO 23950)

ANSI TCP/IP includes over 100 individual protocols. Of particular importance are Telnet, FTP, and SMTP. Telnet (Terminal Emulation Link Network) allows remote users to log on to other network host computers. FTP (File Transfer Protocol) supports the transfer of files from one computer to another. SMTP (Simple Mail Transfer Protocol) supports e-mail messaging via the Internet. Because most e-mail is sent via the Internet, the SMTP protocol has supplanted the IEEE Electronic Messaging (x.400) standard as the most popular e-mail protocol for general use.

NISO Z39/50/ISO 23950, popularly known as Z39.50, allows searches initiated in one system to be transmitted to and executed in another system and responses returned to the original system. This standard opens the doors to the world of information by allowing users to tap the resources of collections and databases located outside the four walls of their local library, using the search syntax of their local system.

UNDERSTANDING TEXTUAL, IMAGE, MULTIMEDIA, AND CD-ROM FILE STANDARDS

Automated systems in libraries have traditionally provided circulation control and electronic card catalogs. As we stated at the beginning of the book, all this is changing with the digitization not just of textual resources but also of pictures, sound, and full-motion video. Libraries now expect their automated systems not just to point to information but also to be the gateways and portals through which the information itself flows. This new focus requires a whole new set of standards, many of which are still in development, which leaves de facto standards to be used in the interim.

These standards include formats for transmission of graphic and full-motion images, markup languages for the creation of electronic documents, and information exchange formats for CD-ROM hardware and software. They are:

- Graphics Interchange Format (GIF)
- Tagged Image File Format (TIFF)
- Portable Document Format (PDF)
- Digital Compression and Coding of Continuous-Tone Still Images (JPEG—Joint Photographic Experts Group; ISO/IEC 10918.1)
- Motion Picture Experts Group (MPEG)
- Standard Generalized Markup Language (SGML; ISO 8879)
- Electronic Manuscript Preparation and Markup (ISO 12083)
- HyperText Markup Language (HTML; W3C HTML 4.01)
- Extended Markup Language (XML; W3C XML)
- Electronic Data Interchange for Administration, Commerce, and Transport (ISO OSI 9735)
- Common Gateway Interface (CGI)
- Volume & File Structure of CD-ROM for Information Exchange (ISO 9660).

These standards, both official and de facto, are important because any library wishing to provide a gateway to and a presence on the World Wide Web must ensure that its automated system conforms to and supports these protocols. Similarly, transparent access to CD-ROM applications, both multimedia and bibliographic, requires compliance with the CD-ROM information exchange standard.

The EDIFACT standard for online communication and ordering from book jobbers, subscription agents, and publishers has been more widely adopted in Europe than in North America, where BISAC and EDI x12 have been more popular. However, NISO has accepted EDIFACT as a replacement for BISAC and it is generally agreed that EDIFACT will supersede EDI x12. It is possible that a further revision of the EDIFACT standard may occur that incorporates elements of both EDI and XML. This is clearly a standard in transition.

DISCERNING E-BOOK STANDARDS: WORKS IN PROGRESS

E-books (electronic books)—digitized content, both textual and pictorial—are an exciting concept being embraced by the reading public and by libraries. E-books are being read on PCs, laptops, PDAs, and proprietary e-book readers. However, there is at the present time no compatibility among e-book readers and there are at least 18 file formats for e-book contents. The development of standards and specifications for these new electronic resources is critical for both publishers and users if e-books are to remain an essential part of library collections and not become mere electronic curiosities.

While there are no formalized standards at present, Z39.86, the ANSI/NISO "File Specification for the Digital Talking Book" is in draft format with approval likely by mid–2001. Meanwhile, several other efforts are underway to address additional e-book standards, attempting to balance the need for interoperability with the desire for an open standard designed to encourage continuing development and innovation.

These works in progress include:

- Open ebook Publication Structure (OeBF; Open ebook Forum)
- Open Ebook Standards Project (American Association of Publishers)
- Electronic Book Exchange (EBX; EBX Working Group)
- Onix International (International Publishers organizations)

The e-book world is one that is changing quickly and constantly. The development of standards, how they will be managed, and who will drive their development will ultimately define how these tools are adopted and used in the coming years.

CONCLUSION

Many of the standards discussed in this chapter have been in existence for years. Some are still in the planning stages. It is important to understand that even the most stable standard, such as MARC, will undergo change over time.

Sometimes a standard will be superseded or replaced by another standard, such as occurred with the standards for holdings statements for serial and nonserial items. Some standards are so new they can't be effectively applied, as is the case currently with the efforts to develop standards for e-books. While you must be aware of shifts and changes in the standards world, that there are shifts and changes doesn't change the fact that adhering to standards is critically important when selecting and implementing an automated system. Standards are your first line of defense against incompatibility between and among systems. Their importance cannot be overemphasized.

SOURCES

Boss, Richard W. 2000. "Information Technology Standards." *Library Technology Reports* 36, no. 4 (July-August): 7–112.
    This updated edition of Boss's 1996 "Standards for Automated Library Systems and Other Information Technologies" retains the same format, but provides updated information on a wide array of standards important to libraries and useful for writing standards specifications in procurement documents. Chapter 1 defines "standards," reviews their role, and describes the major standards organizations. Chapters 2 through 7 discuss specific standards. Chapter 8 specifies language for inclusion in RFPs. Also included are a glossary, a bibliography, and a list of NISO voting members.

Information Standards Quarterly. Bethesda, Md.: National Information Standards Association, published quarterly.
    Articles on emerging and existing standards and standards status reports make this a useful tool. Some information is duplicated on the NISO Web site.

Library of Congress. *Standards*. March 24, 2000 [Online]. Available: http://lcweb.loc.gov/standards/ [2001, April 7].
    This comprehensive Web site provides information on the MARC formats, Digital Library Standards, Z39.50 Retrieval Protocol, Encoded Archival Description (EAD), ISO Language Codes, International Standard Serial Num-

ber (ISSN), Standards in the Library of Congress Collections, and links to related standards organizations.

National Information Standards Organization. Last update unknown [Online]. Available: www.niso.org [2001, April 7].
This Web site has information on NISO's organization, the latest information on the status of draft standards, and a link to TechStreet *(www.techstreet. com/nisogate.html)* where NISO standards and technical reports can be downloaded for free.

"Perspectives on . . . Information Technology Standards." 1992. *Journal of the American Society for Information Science* 43, no. 8 (September): 521–578.
This entire issue of *JASIS* is devoted to "the current work and thinking on information technology standardization—from Z39.50 to X.25, from acid-free paper standards to the growth of SGML and Z39.59." The articles offer "perspectives from both academics and practitioners, with a multidisciplinary focus."

Terry, Ana Arias. 2000. "Ebook Frenzy: An Overview of Issues, Standards, and the Industry." *Information Standards Quarterly* 12, no. 4 (October): 1–7.
This is an excellent overview of the evolving e-book standards. Several emerging standards are analyzed and discussed.

CONCLUSION: PLANNING FOR THE FUTURE

Planning has gained such widespread acceptance in the profession that experience and familiarity with planning can truly be considered an essential skill for every librarian. Planning process methodologies are now the norm in corporations, education, and government, and librarians must master planning concepts and techniques if they are to function effectively within their parent organizations and funding environments.

As we have discussed, plans must be regularly revisited and updated as the environment and needs change. In general, a library should review its plans annually and conduct a major reexamination of its plans every three years. Luckily, this is facilitated because virtually every library prepares some form of report for its public, funding authority, or parent organization on an annual basis. By incorporating a planning review into this process, annual reports can move from a statement of past accomplishments to an opportunity to make others aware of your goals and objectives and to lay the groundwork for your funding request.

An annual review of the technologies that support your goals should be part of this review process because, like your three-year plan, technologies change with time.

IS THERE A LIFE CYCLE FOR AUTOMATED SYSTEMS AND TECHNOLOGY?

THE BAD NEWS: OBSOLESCENCE

As we have come to understand, computer technology and software applications evolve at an incredibly rapid pace. What we said in the previous editions of this book remains true: At current rates of development, you can expect that by the time you install your carefully planned system, capabilities will be available that were only in planning stages while you were evaluating vendor proposals. In computing technology, there is a cynical maxim: "If it works, it must be obsolete."

How long can you expect to be happy with your new system before changes in technology and functionality will render it "obsolete"? In the past, a life cycle of five years was considered acceptable for a computer system before some significant upgrade—installation of additional hardware or software providing for increased capability or capacity—or replacement became necessary. Today, it is inconceivable that a system will last five years before you have to make major changes. It may not "break," in the industrial sense. But current trends suggest that without major changes in perhaps three years or less, your present system will have less power and capability than the computer in a child's bedroom. You must also consider the rapid changes occurring in the telecommunications field and the formulation and reformulation of standards designed to strengthen system performance and interconnectivity.

Accordingly, libraries must not give their parent organizations or funding authorities the impression that planning for and implementing automation is a "one-shot" proposition. From the first, policymakers must be educated to realize that advances in computer and information technology represent a fundamental change in the way libraries do business and require an ongoing commitment to keep pace with a world that is becoming different in fundamental ways from what we have always known.

As our users, whether corporate executives, researchers, distance learners, students, and the public at large, expect more and more to access the *world*—never mind the library—anywhere, anytime, our systems must remain flexible and robust enough to respond. No system lasts forever—but why would we want it to . . . ?

THE GOOD NEWS: IMPROVED SERVICE

This leads us to the positive side of the picture, which is that, due to rapid advances in technology, we are experiencing a tremendous increase in our ability to access, store, and process information. What began with "automating" backroom processes has evolved to the ubiquity of powerful workstations on people's desktops. Future developments that we identified in the second edition of *Planning for Automation* are no longer projections; they are realities to one degree or another.

- There has been an exponential growth in the number of individuals and organizations using electronic technology not only to access but to produce vast amounts of information in a myriad of formats that would never have existed or been accessible in a print environment.

- For the foreseeable future, libraries will remain print oriented overall. However, major shifts are occurring as libraries depend more and more on Web-based resources, electronic journals, digitized collections, and computer-enabled user services of all kinds to meet their customers' expectations.
- There exists far greater interactivity between and among integrated systems. This not only improves access to information and changes individual local systems into "nodes" on the expanding Internet, but also blurs the lines, from our users' perspective, between what one library "has" and what other libraries "have."
- In a concomitant development, library users and staff are gaining greater control over the access tools in libraries, shaping previously static devices such as catalogs (card or computer) into individually customizable front-ends to their library's (and other libraries') information resources.
- Traditional library functions are no longer discrete modules that you buy or not when you acquire a system. They are processes along a continuum of functionality within automated systems, reflecting the blending and merging that is taking place in almost all phases of the work that we do.
- Librarians themselves are starting to play a greater role in the creation, packaging, and distribution of information, adding greater value to the material they make available to their users.
- Library users are availing themselves of a growing number of service enhancements that are allowing them to interact in fundamentally different ways not only with the library but with the materials they are finding and using. Customized files and individualized responses to selectively acquired resources are enabling users to shape what they find to meet their needs in newer, more creative ways.

Remember: With every step you take, you are one step closer to bringing these exciting possibilities and capabilities to your users—and you are gaining valuable experience and knowledge that will promote more effective planning and decision making in the future.

APPRECIATING THE BENEFITS OF GOOD PLANNING

In summary, the results of good planning are:

- confidence that you have selected the *best possible system* available, given technological and financial constraints
- confidence that you have addressed the *priority needs* of your library
- confidence that you have established a firm basis of understanding and a methodology (the planning process) for *future planning*
- confidence on the part of your parent organization or funding authority that technologies are being implemented as part of a clearly articulated, overall plan for the *development of library services*
- confidence that you have the ability to respond quickly and effectively to *unexpected opportunities and challenges* in technology and in other areas, with a clear understanding of how these unexpected developments and technological changes may be used to support the library's long-range goals

APPENDIX: WORKING WITH CONSULTANTS

WHY HIRE A CONSULTANT?

Many libraries engaged in technology planning will at one time or another consider securing the services of a consultant. A technology consultant will function in one or more of the following capacities:

- *Objective Outsider/Authority:* The consultant is employed as an expert who will examine the library and its operations and recommend actions. If the consultant is a recognized authority, his recommendations may be more easily accepted by a funding agency or parent organization.
- *Technical Advisor:* The consultant works with library planners to provide specific information on the technical aspects of implementing technology-based solutions, integrated system capabilities, or evaluation of vendor proposals, thereby supporting the decision-making process rather than making decisions.
- *Trainer/Educator:* The consultant educates planners and parent organization members through a series of structured training activities, providing planners with the technical knowledge they need to make decisions.
- *Process Leader:* The consultant provides a structure for one or more parts of the planning process, supporting group decision-making processes. Examples might include working with staff to develop and prioritize needs, develop specifications, or evaluate proposals.
- *Task Manager:* The consultant is hired to complete a specific task, such as a shelflist analysis, writing a request for proposal, or a bar-code labeling project. The consultant's involvement ends when the task is completed.

It is often useful to retain a consultant early in the planning process to give staff and planners an overview of technology concepts and options and the technology planning process. In many instances, consulting of this type is available from state agencies or consortia at little or no cost. Alternatively, staff may be able to attend continuing education programs and seminars offered off-site through professional agencies, state agencies, consortia, or consultants. Either way, remember to have as many staff as possible participate. Education is a modest expense that will yield real returns throughout the planning process.

If you intend to utilize a consultant in the system selection process, it is best if you also involve the consultant in the development of system specifications and identification of priorities (see below). That way, the consultant will have a firm understanding of the library's needs when the selection is made.

FINDING AND SELECTING A CONSULTANT

If your library has decided to use a consultant, the first thing you will need to do is develop a written description of what the consultant will do. Keeping in mind the roles outlined earlier, this description should include:

- steps of the planning process in which the consultant will be involved
- the consultant's responsibilities at each step
- meetings the consultant will attend and with whom the consultant will meet (on-site consulting days)
- written or oral reports the consultant will present and to whom they will be presented
- a desired timeline for the above activities
- a request for a cost proposal, a statement of qualifications, and a list of previous clients

This document should then be distributed to appropriate consultants. Names of potential consultants may be garnered from professional associations and from state and cooperative library agencies and directories. Your library may also advertise its interest in receiving proposals in one or more appropriate professional publications with wide distribution.

Normally, the result of your efforts will be the receipt of one or more proposals from consultants. In selecting the consultant, the following criteria should be kept in mind:

1. the degree to which the consultant's proposal matches your requirements
2. the consultant's experience in assisting similar libraries with similar projects
3. positive evaluations from previous clients
4. proposed costs

To standardize the evaluation process, those involved in selecting the consultant should give each proposal a rating based on each of the criteria. This will help make the selection process more objective—and it provides good practice for the *system* selection process. Once the field has been narrowed down, a meeting with each candidate (if possible) will assist your planning committee in assessing such factors as style and interpersonal skills.

FORMULATING THE CONSULTANT AGREEMENT

Once you have selected your consultant, you must confirm in writing all of the specifics included in your proposal and in the response. At a minimum, a letter should specify the number of on-site consulting days, any reports to be provided, and the total cost of services to be provided. It also can be useful to agree on a per diem rate for additional work that the library may wish the consultant to provide later on in the planning process. With clear requirements and a specific written agreement, both you and your consultant should have the same expectations.

CONSIDERING ETHICAL ISSUES IN TECHNOLOGY CONSULTING

As the library-consultant relationship develops, all parties should remain aware of important standards of behavior that will enhance the outcome of the consultation process. A few of these, with particular relevance to technology consulting, may be outlined as follows:

1. The client library has a responsibility to maintain a proper and correct relationship with prospective consultants and with the consultant it selects. This includes:
   - preparing an accurate and complete RFP—one that fully presents the library's technology-related purposes in retaining a consultant's services
   - genuinely seeking its consultant's expertise and recommendations in an open decision-making process, that is, the library has not already made its decisions
   - moving ahead with decisions, system requirements, and the like that represent the work that has been done and not making alterations without informing the consultant
   - remembering that materials developed by the library's consultant are proprietary

2. The consultant has a responsibility to maintain her objectivity and lack of bias throughout the process. This means:
   - honestly representing her skills, background, and references in any response to an RFP for consulting services
   - cooperating with the client library but not acquiescing when, in her best professional judgment, the library's expectations are counterproductive to the process
   - working to develop a solution that meets the library's needs as opposed to offering a favorite solution out of context
   - being open about any relationships she may have with a prospective system or other technology vendor and not concealing any potential conflicts of interest

3. Both the client library and the consultant have a responsibility to:
   - ensure an open, honest process in securing vendor services for technology. Most especially, this means not "wiring a bid," that is, preparing an inherently biased RFP or similar document that wastes the time and efforts of vendors responding in good faith but who, in reality, have been excluded before the fact
   - maintain confidentiality on all matters pertaining to the consultation, particularly when a competitive process for providing services or systems is involved
   - maintain a professional relationship at all times, including the avoidance of "finger-pointing" if problems or disagreements develop

MAKING THE MOST OF YOUR CONSULTANT

It is not always possible or desirable to use a consultant. When used effectively, however, consultants can save time, may save money, and may help you feel confident that you are making the best possible decision given the available options.

Libraries often bring unrealistic expectations to consulting situations. More realistic expectations and an understanding of consultant roles will help prevent disappointment and ensure the most effective results when you do use a consultant. *Consultants cannot and should not take the place of active administrative and staff involvement in the automation planning process.*

If you use a consultant, keep in mind that the consultant's job is not to make the decision for you, but to assist you in obtaining background and technical information and establishing a structure within which you can make your own decisions. After all, you and your staff understand your library and its patrons better than any consultant can hope to. And in the long run, the most successful technology planning is based on decisions made by the library's staff. The long process of education, prioritization, identification of alternatives, evaluation, and selection will be the best guarantee of satisfaction with the results.

SOURCES

Garten, Edward D., ed. 1992. *Using Consultants in Libraries and Information Centers: A Management Handbook*. Westport, Conn.: Greenwood.
Essays explore establishing the reasons for using a consultant, processes for ensuring a successful consulting relationship, using a consultant for various purposes, ethical issues and dilemmas, and alternative methods for securing consulting expertise. In particular, Edwin M. Cortez and Susan Baerg Epstein, respectively, write about the role of consultants in the development of RFPs and in contract negotiations. M.E.L. Jacob discusses using consultants in the strategic planning process.

Holtz, Herman. 1989. *Choosing and Using a Consultant: A Manager's Guide to Consulting Services*. New York: Wiley.
This book covers how to know when you need a consultant (assessing your need), how to find consultants, soliciting and evaluating bids, negotiations, and cost guidelines. Deals with common problems, how to maintain good relations, and the final evaluation of your consultant's work.

Matthews, Joseph R. 1994. "The Effective Use of Consultants in Libraries." *Library Technology Reports* 30, no. 6 (November/December): 745–814.
This "Report" within *LTR* reviews all aspects of finding, hiring, and working with a consultant. There is a section on codes of practice, guidelines, and standards (pp. 767–778).

McNamara, Carter. "All About Using Consultants." 1999 [Online]. Available: www.mapnp.org/library/misc/cnsltng.htm [2001, March 6].
This site covers situations when a consultant is useful, where to get consultants, making a consultant relationship as productive as possible, and hiring the consultant. There are useful links to a sample RFP for consulting services, a sample "Proposed Consultation Plan," and a sample "Contract for services."

"RFPs Should Reflect Realistic Goals." 1994. *Library Systems Newsletter* 14, no. 2 (February): 10–12.
This letter from an established consultant to a city purchasing department regarding its RFP for consulting services underscores some of the pitfalls that libraries should avoid when developing procurement documents for professional services.

Schroll, R. Craig. "Consultants: A Brief Guide to Effective Selection & Use." No date [Online]. Available: http://siri.uvm.edu/library/consultants.html [2001, March 6].
This site focuses on the finding and selecting of consultants, getting results, then evaluating the project. The discussion includes brief checklist-style questions on these topics.

Shenson, Howard L. 1990. *How to Select and Manage Consultants: A Guide to Getting What You Pay For*. Lexington, Mass.: D.C. Heath.
The author discusses consultant roles, finding and evaluating consultants, fees, proposals, and contracts. Sample consultant proposals and letters of agreement are included, as is a critical, annotated bibliography.

INDEX

ABOUT THE AUTHORS

John M. Cohn and Ms. Ann L. Kelsey are Director and Associate Director respectively of the Sherman H. Masten Learning Resource Center at the County College of Morris in Randolph, New Jersey, and partners in DocuMentors, an independent consulting firm. Mr. Keith Michael Fiels is Director of the Massachusetts Board of Library Commissioners in Boston.

Previous Neal-Schuman books coauthored by Dr. Cohn, Ms. Kelsey, and Mr. Fiels include *Writing and Updating Technology Plans: A Guidebook with Sample Plans on CD-ROM* (2000) and *Planning for Automation: A How-To-Do-It Manual for Librarians* (2nd ed., 1997; 1st ed., 1992).